CAMBRIDGE NATIONAL LEVEL 1/LEVEL 2

Engineering Design

Revision Guide and Workbook

Claire Reet

CAMBRIDGE
UNIVERSITY PRESS

University Printing House, Cambridge CB2 8BS, United Kingdom

One Liberty Plaza, 20th Floor, New York, NY 10006, USA

477 Williamstown Road, Port Melbourne, VIC 3207, Australia

314–321, 3rd Floor, Plot 3, Splendor Forum, Jasola District Centre, New Delhi – 110025, India

103 Penang Road, #05–06/07, Visioncrest Commercial, Singapore 23846

Cambridge University Press is part of the University of Cambridge.

It furthers the University's mission by disseminating knowledge in the pursuit of education, learning and research at the highest international levels of excellence.

www.cambridge.org
Information on this title: www.cambridge.org/9781009119290

© Cambridge University Press & Assessment 2022

This publication is in copyright. Subject to statutory exception and to the provisions of relevant collective licensing agreements, no reproduction of any part may take place without the written permission of Cambridge University Press & Assessment.

First published 2022

20 19 18 17 16 15 14 13 12 11 10 9 8 7 6 5 4 3 2

Printed in Poland by Opolgraf

A catalogue record for this publication is available from the British Library

ISBN 978-1-009-11929-0 Paperback with Digital Access (2 Years)
ISBN 978-1-009-11329-8 Digital Revision Guide and Workbook (2 Years)
ISBN 978-1-009-11330-4 Site Licence (1 Year)

Additional resources for this publication at www.cambridge.org/go/

Cambridge University Press has no responsibility for the persistence or accuracy of URLs for external or third-party internet websites referred to in this publication, and does not guarantee that any content on such websites is, or will remain, accurate or appropriate. Information regarding prices, travel timetables, and other factual information given in this work is correct at the time of first printing but Cambridge University Press does not guarantee the accuracy of such information thereafter.

....

NOTICE TO TEACHERS IN THE UK
It is illegal to reproduce any part of this work in material form (including photocopying and electronic storage) except under the following circumstances:
(i) where you are abiding by a licence granted to your school or institution by the Copyright Licensing Agency;
(ii) where no such licence exists, or where you wish to exceed the terms of a licence, and you have gained the written permission of Cambridge University Press;
(iii) where you are allowed to reproduce without permission under the provisions of Chapter 3 of the Copyright, Designs and Patents Act 1988, which covers, for example, the reproduction of short passages within certain types of educational anthology and reproduction for the purposes of setting examination questions.

....

Contents

Preparing for the exam

Your Revision Guide and Workbook	4
Planning your revision	5
Revision techniques	7
Getting ready for the exam	9
What to expect in the exam	10
Revision checklist	16

Unit R038: Principles of engineering design

Revision Guide

TA1:	Designing processes	19
TA2:	Design requirements	33
TA3:	Communicating design outcomes	45
TA4:	Evaluating design ideas	58

Workbook

TA1:	Designing processes	71
TA2:	Design requirements	79
TA3:	Communicating design outcomes	88
TA4:	Evaluating design ideas	94

Glossary

Key terms	98
Command words	102

Answers

Answers to 'Practise it!' activities	103
Answers to Workbook questions	105

Acknowledgements   111

Preparing for the exam

Your Revision Guide and Workbook

This Revision Guide will support you in preparing for the exam for Unit R038 Principles of engineering design. This is the externally assessed unit of your course.

The Revision Guide contains two types of pages, as shown below:

- Content pages to help you revise the content you need to know
- Workbook pages with practice exam-style questions to help you prepare for your exam.

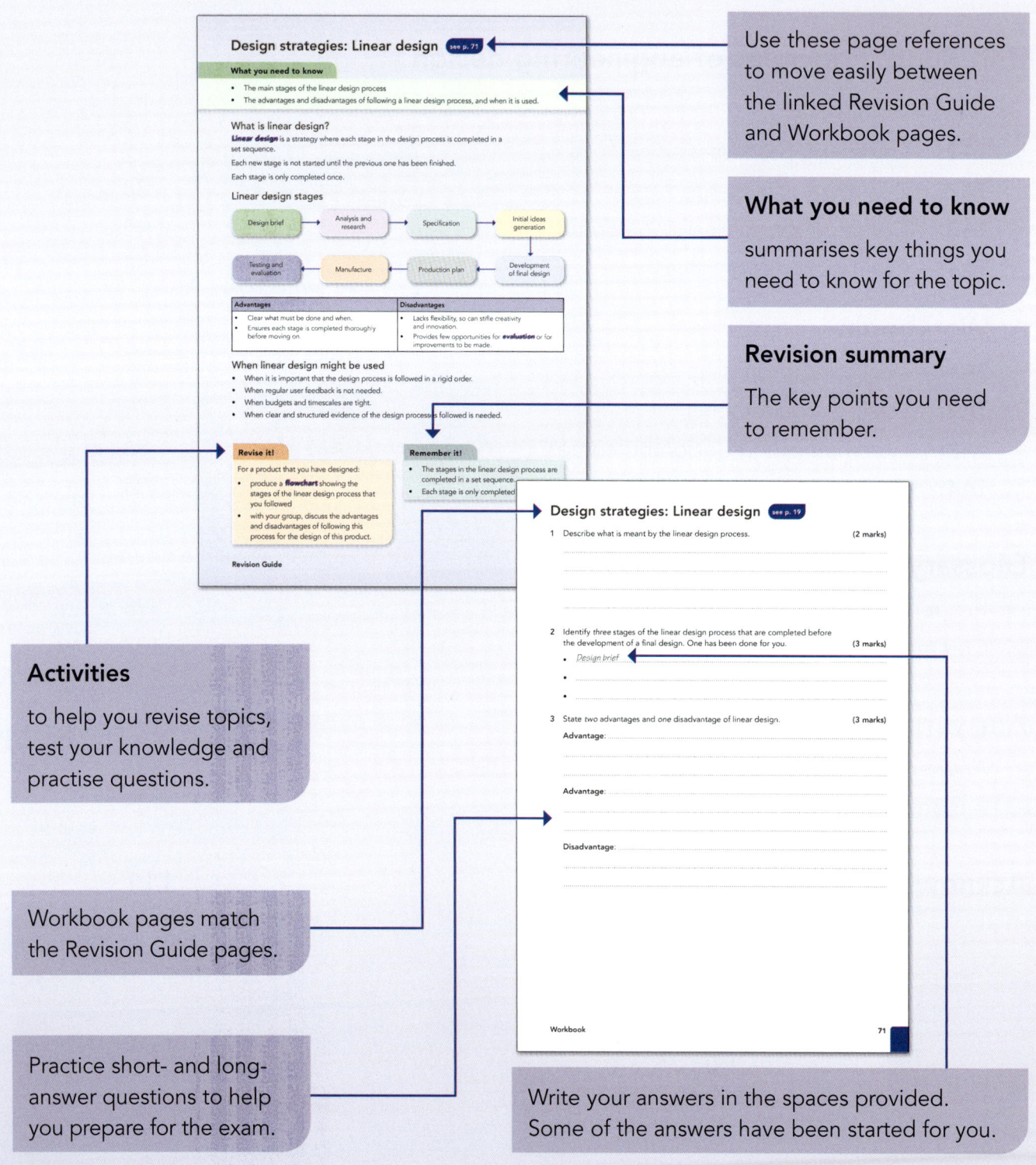

Use these page references to move easily between the linked Revision Guide and Workbook pages.

What you need to know
summarises key things you need to know for the topic.

Revision summary
The key points you need to remember.

Activities
to help you revise topics, test your knowledge and practise questions.

Workbook pages match the Revision Guide pages.

Practice short- and long-answer questions to help you prepare for the exam.

Write your answers in the spaces provided. Some of the answers have been started for you.

4 Preparing for the exam

Planning your revision

Countdown to the exam

Revision checklists are a good way for you to plan and structure your revision.
They also allow you to make sure you have covered everything you need to cover:

Revision planner checklist

Time before the exam	Things to do	
6–8 weeks	• Draw up a revision timetable so that you know how much time you have to get through everything.	☐
	• Use the revision checklist on page 16 to work out which topics you need to cover. Look back at how well you did on past paper questions or other assessments to help you decide what you need to work on.	☐
	• Use the topic area headings and bullets to organise your notes and to make sure you've covered everything in the specification.	☐
	• Don't spend too much time each day revising; quality, spaced revision is better than studying all day every day.	☐
4–6 weeks	• Work out which of the areas you still find difficult and plan when you'll cover them.	☐
	• You may be able to discuss tricky topics with your teacher or class colleagues.	☐
	• As you feel you've got to grips with some of the knowledge, you can 'tick off' the parts that have been worrying you.	☐
	• Make the most of the revision sessions you're offered in class. Don't skip them!	☐
1 week	• Make a daily plan to revise those few topics you're not happy with and look back at your revision cards (see below) if you've made some.	☐
Day before	• Try not to cram today – get some exercise and relax in the afternoon.	☐
	• Make sure you know what time and where the exam is and put all your things out (pencils, pens, calculator, bus pass, water) ready for the next day.	☐
	• Get a good night's sleep!	☐

Revise it!

Using the example above, create your own revision checklist. Identify areas that you are not so confident about and think of ways to tackle these.

Preparing for the exam

Revision tips

Choose the methods that work for you

For example:
- use highlighters for key words and phrases
- make note cards
- use mnemonics (the first letter of words): for example, 'ACCESS FM' stands for Aesthetics, Cost, Customer, Environment, Size, Safety, Function and Materials.

Plan your revision

Make a list of all the key dates from when you start your revision up to the exam date.

Take breaks

Plan regular breaks in your revision. Go for a short walk or get some fresh air. It will make you more focused when you do revise!

Learn everything!

Questions can be asked about **any area** of the specification.

It is easier to answer a question if you have revised everything.

Don't cram!

Plan to space your revision out so that you don't do everything at once!

Identify your strengths and weaknesses

Complete the 'Revision checklist' at the end of each chapter and identify areas that you feel less confident about. Allow additional time to revise these areas.

Use mind maps!

Mind maps are great for connecting ideas and memorising information more easily and quickly.

Attend revision classes!

Don't skip revision classes – it can really help to revise with your friends as well as by yourself.

Stay healthy!

Exercise, fresh air, good food and staying hydrated all help your revision.

Variety is the spice of life!

Mix up your revision methods. Watch videos and listen to podcasts as well as making notes and mind maps.

Find a quiet space

It can be difficult to revise in loud or busy spaces, so try to find somewhere calm to work. You could use headphones and music to block out distractions.

Preparing for the exam

Revision techniques

Flash cards/revision cards

These are useful for summarising content, key word definitions and important facts. Use colours to make certain things stand out – for example, you could use different colours for advantages and disadvantages or for key words. You can test yourself using the revision cards.

Mind maps

These are a really useful visual summary of information and you can put them on the wall. They allow you to show links between ideas and concepts. You can start by adding the topic to the centre of the diagram and then add the sub-topics around that and a summary of the information.

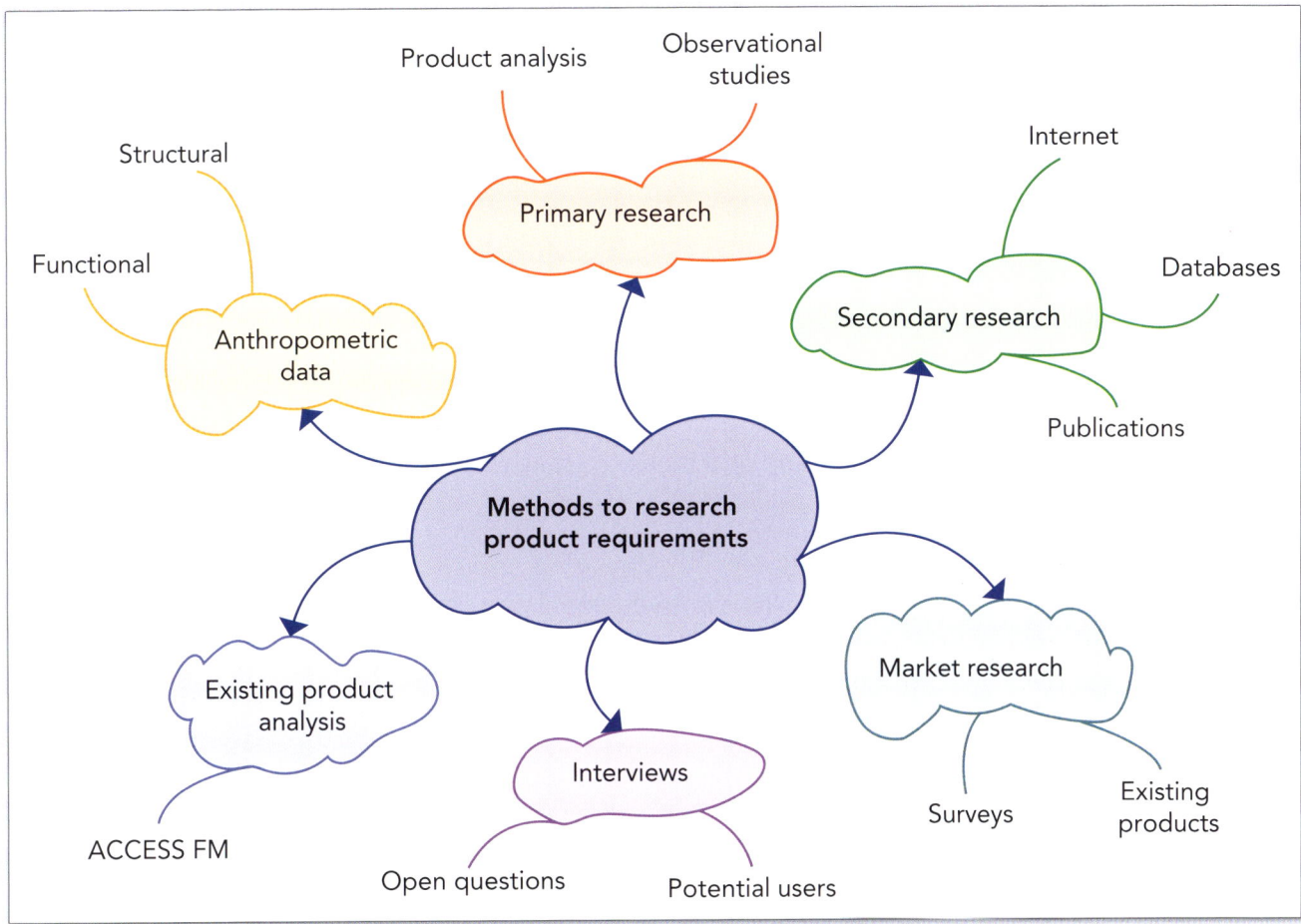

Revise it!

Create a mind map for a topic of your choice.

Preparing for the exam

Highlighting

Making notes and highlighting key areas to go back to is a good way of working out what you know and don't know. You can then use these notes as you come to your final revision. You can use different colours to highlight different factors or different types of information. For example, when revising the different research methods, you could colour-code which methods are primary and which methods are secondary.

Summaries

On the revision pages of this book, you'll find summaries of key ideas and themes. Use these to help you summarise the key points you'll need to remember to answer questions on those topics. For example, you need to know different processes used to model. You can make a summary of these yourself – and if you think through these points in the exam, you are more likely to remember them.

Mnemonics

A mnemonic is another useful way of remembering key facts by using the first letter of each of the parts to make up a memorable phrase. For example, 'ACCESS FM' stands for Aesthetics, Cost, Customer, Environment, Size, Safety, Function and Materials.

Quizzes

Everyone enjoys quizzes and creating and sharing quizzes with your friends and class is a great way to remember facts and concepts. You could suggest to your teacher that in pairs you create a quiz of ten questions and each week go through them together – swapping answers. It's also a good way for you to check your knowledge. Make a note of the areas where you really didn't know the answer and add these to your revision list.

Practice questions

Trying past papers and practice exam questions is an essential part of your revision. It prepares you for answering different types of exam questions and allows you to become familiar with the wording of the questions used by OCR.

You should also use the mark scheme. This will help you understand how to get full marks for each question.

It is helpful to highlight key words in exam questions so you're clear what the question is asking before you answer it.

Getting ready for the exam

Use the revision checklist and all your revision material to make sure you are as prepared as possible. Do plenty of practice with exam questions and quick quizzes.

In the exam

Give yourself time to complete the whole paper, and check through it for mistakes. Most importantly, try to stay calm and relaxed – remember, this is your time to show off what you know!

Get plenty of sleep

Make sure you get a good night's sleep the night before the exam. Don't stay up late cramming as you need time to switch off and relax before going to bed.

Keep hydrated but don't drink too much

It's important that you stay hydrated but don't overdo it or else you'll be running to the toilet. Exams can make you a bit nervous too which means you might need to go to the toilet a bit more frequently. Water is best.

Eat a good, healthy meal

Have a good, healthy meal that you enjoy the night before the exam and a filling breakfast on the day of the exam to give you a boost ready for your exam.

Make sure you have all the things you need

Get everything ready the night before – including all writing equipment, a calculator if you need one (and are allowed one), a water bottle, tissues if you have a sniff, and any identification you might need (candidate number if you have been given one).

Getting ready for the exam

Set your alarm

If your exam is in the morning, set an alarm *or two* so you have plenty of time to get to the exam. If you're still worried about oversleeping, ask a friend or someone in your family to make sure you're up.

Arrive in plenty of time

Know when and where the exam is. Get there at least 15 minutes before it starts. If your exam is in an unfamiliar part of the school and away from where you normally study, you might have to leave home a bit earlier. Don't be distracted on the way!

Don't be tempted to do too much cramming

Too much last-minute cramming can scramble your brain! You may find that being relaxed will help you recall the facts you need rather than attempting last minute cramming, but you may also want to revise the key facts before setting off for the exam.

Preparing for the exam

What to expect in the exam

As part of your qualification in Engineering Design you will be taking an exam that is worth 40 percent of your marks. It is important that from the beginning you start to think about the exam and the skills you'll need to get the best possible grade. Answering exam questions is a skill. Like any other skill, it can be learnt, practised and improved.

Below is an outline of what to expect in the exam, the types of questions and what the paper looks like. You need to answer all the questions.

Types of questions to expect in the exam

Exam questions can be asked about any area of the specification, which means that you have to learn everything!

The exam paper will be made up of two sections, with different types of questions.

Question type	Description
Multiple-choice question (MCQ)	• A question with four answer options • Worth 1 mark
Short-answer question	• Usually require a one-word answer or a simple sentence • Worth 1–4 marks
Long-answer question	• Open response question where you are expected to do a piece of extended writing • Worth up to 8 marks • These questions allow you to be assessed on the quality of your written communication

Understanding the language of the exam

The command word is the key term that tells you how to answer the question. It is essential to know what the different command words mean and what they are asking you to do. It is easy to confuse the words and provide too much information, not enough information or the wrong information. The tables below will help you understand what each command word is asking you to do.

Command words that ask you to get creative

Command word	OCR definition	How you should approach it
Create	• Produce a visual solution to a problem (for example: a mind map, flowchart or visualisation).	Show your answer in a visual way. You might want to use a mind map, flowchart or a diagram. Think about what is the best way to show the required information.
Draw	• Produce a picture or diagram.	Create a picture/diagram to show the relevant information.

Command words that ask you to choose the correct answer

Command word	OCR definition	How you should approach it
Choose	• Select an answer from options given.	Pick the option that you think is correct.
Circle	• Select an answer from options given.	Draw a circle around the correct answer.
Identify	• Select an answer from options given. • Recognise, name or provide factors or features.	Either choose the correct answer from those given or write the name, factors or features that are asked for.

Command words that ask you to add to something

Command word	OCR definition	How you should approach it
Annotate	• Add information, for example, to a table, diagram or graph until it is final. • Add all the needed or appropriate parts.	Add short notes to the table/diagram/graph to say what each part is.
Complete	• Add all the needed or appropriate parts. • Add information, for example, to a table, diagram or graph until it is final.	Add the information that is missing. Often you will need to give just one word as an answer but sometimes you may need to write more. You may need to finish drawing a diagram or graph.
Fill in	• Add all the needed or appropriate parts. • Add information, for example, to a table, diagram or graph until it is final.	Add the information that is missing. Often you will need to give just one word as an answer but sometimes you may need to write more.
Label	• Add information, for example, to a table, diagram or graph until it is final. • Add all the necessary or appropriate parts.	This often refers to a diagram or a picture. Add words or short phrases to say what each part is. You could add arrows next to your label that point to the right part of the diagram/graph.

Command words that ask you to do your maths

Command word	OCR definition	How you should approach it
Calculate	• Get a numerical answer showing how it has been worked out.	Do your maths. Give the final answer but make sure you show how you got there.

Command words that ask you to give the main points

Command word	OCR definition	How you should approach it
Outline	• Give a short account, summary or description.	Write about the main points. Don't write lots of detailed information.
State	• Give factors or features. • Give short, factual answers.	Give a short answer that names factors or features of something. Sometimes you will be asked to give a certain number of factors/features.

Command words that ask you to be factual

Command word	OCR definition	How you should approach it
Describe	• Give an account including all the relevant characteristics, qualities or events. • Give a detailed account of.	This is the 'what'. Write about **what** something is.
Explain	• Give reasons for and/or causes of. • Use the words or phrases such as 'because', 'therefore' or 'this means that' in answers.	This is the 'how' and the 'why'. Write about **how** something happens or works and **why** it does.

Preparing for the exam

Command words that ask you to give an opinion

Command word	OCR definition	How you should approach it
Analyse	• Separate or break down information into parts and identify its characteristics or elements. • Explain the pros and cons of a topic or argument and make reasoned comments. • Explain the impacts of actions using a logical chain of reasoning.	This term wants you to write about the details. Write about each part in turn, giving key information and saying what is good or bad about it.
Compare and contrast	• Give an account of the similarities and differences between two or more items or situations.	'Compare' means to say what is the **same** about two (or more) things. 'Contrast' means to say what is **different** about two (or more) things.
Discuss	• Present, analyse and evaluate relevant points (for example, for/against an argument).	Write about something in detail, including its strengths and weaknesses. Say what you think about each side of the argument. You don't need to take a side.
Evaluate	• Make a reasoned qualitative judgement considering different factors and using available knowledge/experience.	Write down the arguments for and against something. Then give your opinion about which is the strongest argument.
Justify	• Give good reasons for offering an opinion or reaching a conclusion.	Write what you think would be the best option and say why you think this. Give evidence to support your answer.

> **Practise it!**
>
> Now go to www.cambridge.org/go/ and complete the practice questions on understanding the exam command words.

Common exam mistakes

Common mistakes	Why it matters	Solutions
Not attempting a question	You won't get any marks for a blank answer.	• Answer every question. • Write something – you may pick up a few marks, which can add up to make the difference between grades. • Use your general knowledge. • State the obvious.
Not answering the question that is asked	You won't get any marks for writing about another topic.	• Know what the command words are looking for. • RTQ – read the question. • ATQ – answer the question.
Not providing enough points to achieve the marks	You won't gain full marks.	• Look at the number of marks next to the question – one mark = one point; two marks = two points, three marks = three points, etc.

Answering long-answer questions

Planning your answer

To help you organise your thoughts it is helpful to plan your answer for 8-mark questions. You don't need to take too long. A spider diagram, for example, will help you get your answer in the right order and it makes sure you don't forget anything. For example:

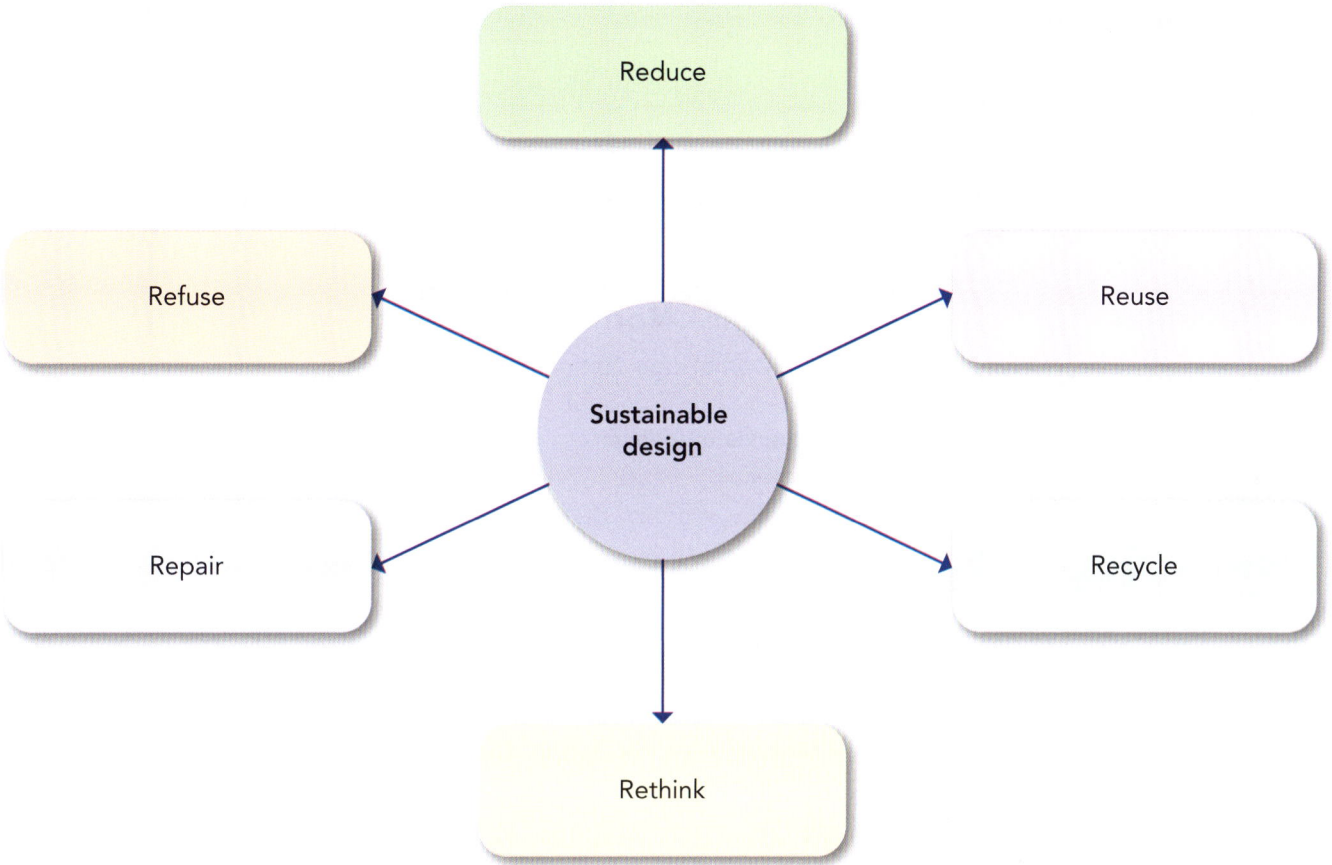

> **Revise it!**
>
> Create a spider diagram plan like the one above for the following question:
>
> > 'Suzanne needs to analyse the following design brief: Design a set of recycling bins to encourage primary children to recycle.
> >
> > Explain the advantages and disadvantages of using this method to analyse a design brief and brainstorm ideas during the research stage of the design process.'
>
> **Tip:** You could refer to page 25 of the Revision Guide to help you.

Preparing for the exam

The exam paper

> Make sure you know how long you have got.

> Write your first name and last name clearly in the box.

> Ensure that you write clear, structured answers so that you can get maximum marks.

OCR
Oxford Cambridge and RSA

Sample Assessment Material (SAM)

...day ... Month Year – Morning/Afternoon

OCR Level 1/Level 2 Cambridge Nationals in Engineering Design

R038: Principles of engineering design

Time allowed: 1 hour 15 minutes

You must have:
- a ruler

You can use:
- a calculator

Write clearly in black ink. **Do not write in the barcodes.**

Centre number ☐☐☐☐☐   Candidate number ☐☐☐☐☐

First name(s) _____
Last name _____

INSTRUCTIONS
- Use black ink.
- Write your answer to each question in the space provided. You can use extra paper if you need to, but you must clearly show your candidate number, the centre number and the question numbers.
- Answer **all** the questions.

INFORMATION
- The total mark for this paper is **70**.
- The marks for each question are shown in brackets **[ ]**.
- Dimensions are in millimeters unless the question says something different.
- This document has **20** pages.

ADVICE
- Read each question carefully before you start your answer.

© OCR 2021 [.../.../...]   OCR is an exempt Charity   **Turn over**
DC (...) 000000
Version 2 (July 2021)

---

14   Preparing for the exam

6

Section B

11 (a) A design brief sets out what is required by a user. State **two** types of information that may be included in a design brief.

1 ....

....

2 ....

....

[2]

> The question is asking for two points. Be sure to give two points in your answer to get full marks.

(b) State **two** aesthetic factors that can influence a user's opinion of a product.

1 ....

....

2 ....

....

[2]

(c) State the meaning of 'market pull'.

....

....

[1]

(d) Explain **one** way in which ergonomic design could improve the use of a computer mouse.

....

....

....

....

[2]

© OCR 2021
Version 2 (July 2021)

> Highlight or underline key words in the question. Here you need to make specific reference to ergonomic design.

> The number of marks indicates the number of points you need to give. In this case, two points are needed.

Preparing for the exam 15

Revision checklist

Topic Area	What you should know			
Topic Area 1: Designing process	**1.1 The stages involved in design strategies**			
	• Design strategies: Linear design	☐	☐	☐
	• Design strategies: Iterative design	☐	☐	☐
	• Design strategies: Inclusive design	☐	☐	☐
	• Design strategies: User-centred design	☐	☐	☐
	• Design strategies: Sustainable design	☐	☐	☐
	• Design strategies: Ergonomic design	☐	☐	☐
	1.2 Stages of the iterative design process, and the activities carried out within each stage of this cyclic approach			
	• Iterative design: Analysis of the design brief	☐	☐	☐
	• Iterative design: Methods of researching the product requirements	☐	☐	☐
	• Iterative design: Producing an engineering design specification	☐	☐	☐
	• Iterative design: Generating design ideas by sketching and modelling	☐	☐	☐
	• Iterative design: Reasons for using modelling	☐	☐	☐
	• Iterative design: Virtual modelling of design ideas	☐	☐	☐
	• Iterative design: Physical modelling	☐	☐	☐
	• Iterative design: Manufacturing or modifying a prototype	☐	☐	☐
Topic Area 2: Design requirements	**2.1 Types of criteria included in an engineering design specification**			
	• Design criteria: Needs and wants	☐	☐	☐
	• Design criteria: Quantitative and qualitative	☐	☐	☐
	• Design criteria: ACCESS FM	☐	☐	☐
	2.2 How manufacturing considerations affect design			
	• Manufacturing considerations: Scale	☐	☐	☐
	• Manufacturing considerations: Availability and form	☐	☐	☐
	• Manufacturing considerations: Processes	☐	☐	☐
	• Manufacturing considerations: Production costs	☐	☐	☐

	2.3 Influences on engineering product design			
	• Influences on product design: Pull and push	☐	☐	☐
	• Influences on product design: Standards	☐	☐	☐
	• Influences on product design: Legislation	☐	☐	☐
	• Influences on product design: Planned obsolescence	☐	☐	☐
	• Influences on product design: Sustainable design and the circular economy	☐	☐	☐
Topic Area 3: Communicating design outcomes	**3.1 Types of drawing used in engineering**			
	• Types of drawing: Freehand and isometric	☐	☐	☐
	• Types of drawing: Oblique and orthographic	☐	☐	☐
	• Types of drawing: Exploded views and assembly drawings	☐	☐	☐
	• Types of drawing: Block diagrams and flowcharts	☐	☐	☐
	• Types of drawing: Circuit diagrams and wiring diagrams	☐	☐	☐
	3.2 Working drawings			
	• Working drawings: Third angle orthographic projection	☐	☐	☐
	• Working drawings: Standard conventions	☐	☐	☐
	• Working drawings: Dimensions	☐	☐	☐
	• Working drawings: Line types	☐	☐	☐
	• Working drawings: Mechanical features	☐	☐	☐
	• Working drawings: Abbreviations	☐	☐	☐
	3.3 Using CAD drawing software			
	• Using CAD drawing software	☐	☐	☐
Topic Area 4: Evaluating design ideas	**4.1 Methods of evaluating design ideas**			
	• Evaluating design ideas: Production of models	☐	☐	☐
	• Evaluating design ideas: Qualitative comparison	☐	☐	☐
	• Evaluating design ideas: Ranking matrices	☐	☐	☐
	• Evaluating design ideas: Quality function deployment	☐	☐	☐

Revision checklist

4.2 Modelling methods			
• Modelling methods: Virtual (3D CAD)	☐	☐	☐
• Modelling methods: Card	☐	☐	☐
• Modelling methods: Block	☐	☐	☐
• Modelling methods: Breadboarding	☐	☐	☐
• Modelling methods: 3D printing	☐	☐	☐
4.3 Methods of evaluating a design outcome			
• Evaluating design outcomes: Dimensions and functionality	☐	☐	☐
• Evaluating design outcomes: Quantitative comparison	☐	☐	☐
• Evaluating design outcomes: User testing	☐	☐	☐
• Evaluating design outcomes: Modifications and improvements	☐	☐	☐

Design strategies: Linear design (see p. 71)

What you need to know
- The main stages of the linear design process
- The advantages and disadvantages of following a linear design process, and when it is used.

What is linear design?
Linear design is a strategy where each stage in the design process is completed in a set sequence.

Each new stage is not started until the previous one has been finished.

Each stage is only completed once.

Linear design stages

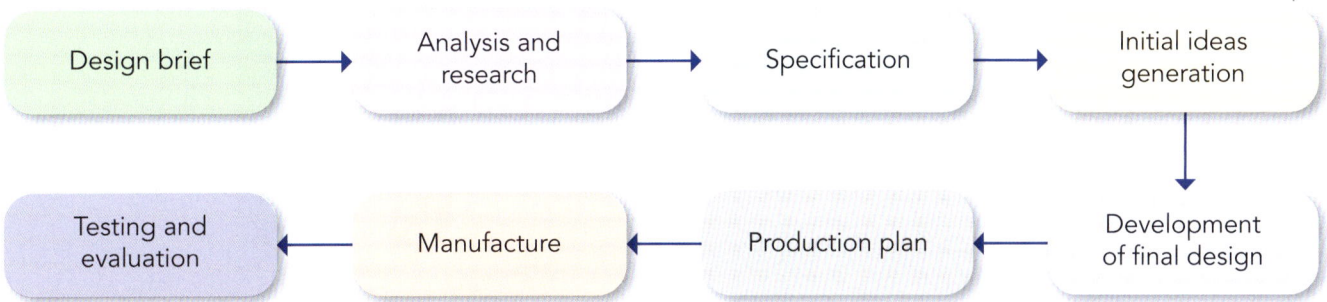

Advantages	Disadvantages
• Clear what must be done and when. • Ensures each stage is completed thoroughly before moving on.	• Lacks flexibility, so can stifle creativity and innovation. • Provides few opportunities for **evaluation** or for improvements to be made.

When linear design might be used
- When it is important that the design process is followed in a rigid order.
- When regular user feedback is not needed.
- When budgets and timescales are tight.
- When clear and structured evidence of the design processes followed is needed.

Revise it!
For a product that you have designed:
- produce a **flowchart** showing the stages of the linear design process that you followed
- with your group, discuss the advantages and disadvantages of following this process for the design of this product.

Remember it!
- The stages in the linear design process are completed in a set sequence.
- Each stage is only completed once.

Design strategies: Iterative design see p. 72

What you need to know

- The main stages of the iterative design process.
- The advantages and disadvantages of following an iterative design process, and when it is used.

What is iterative design?

Most new products are designed using an **iterative design** process. This is a cyclic loop of prototyping, testing and refining ideas.

Iterative design stages

An initial model or prototype is made

This is tested to check how well it meets the needs of the user

The design is evaluated, and an improved iteration is made

The process is repeated until all the requirements of the design have been met. A good example is the first Dyson vacuum cleaner which took more than 5000 **prototypes** to get right!

Advantages	Disadvantages
• Encourages flexibility and creativity. • Errors are found and corrected quickly. • Opportunities for testing, evaluation and feedback.	• Increased cost of resources and time needed. • Requires good oversight to keep designing focused.

When iterative design might be used

- When regular user feedback is required.
- When solving problems that require creative thinking.
- When a clear record of each version of a design is needed.
- When designing products that will be made in large quantities.

Revise it!

- Research some products that have been designed using an iterative process.
- For each, explain why the iterative process was used and the benefits of using it.

Remember it!

- Iterative design is a cyclic process of modelling/prototyping, testing and evaluation.
- Each refinement results in a new iteration of the design.

20 Revision Guide

Design strategies: Inclusive design see p. 73

What you need to know

- What is meant by inclusive design and how it is used.
- The advantages and disadvantages of inclusive design.

It is important for designers to ensure that as many people can use their designs as possible. The process of ensuring this happens is called **inclusive design**.

What is inclusive design?

A **design strategy** that aims to reduce barriers to the use of products.

About ensuring as many people can use a product as possible, without any special modifications.

For example, people with disabilities, older adults or those with particular religious, social or ethical beliefs.

Advantages	Disadvantages
- Ensures nobody feels 'left out' by a design. - Reduces user frustration when using products. - Increases sales of a product.	- Increases cost and time needed for research and development.

Ensuring your design is inclusive

- Get feedback from a wide range of potential users.
- Consider the needs of users who face particular challenges, such as those with disabilities.
- Observe users to see what problems they face and how they could be solved.

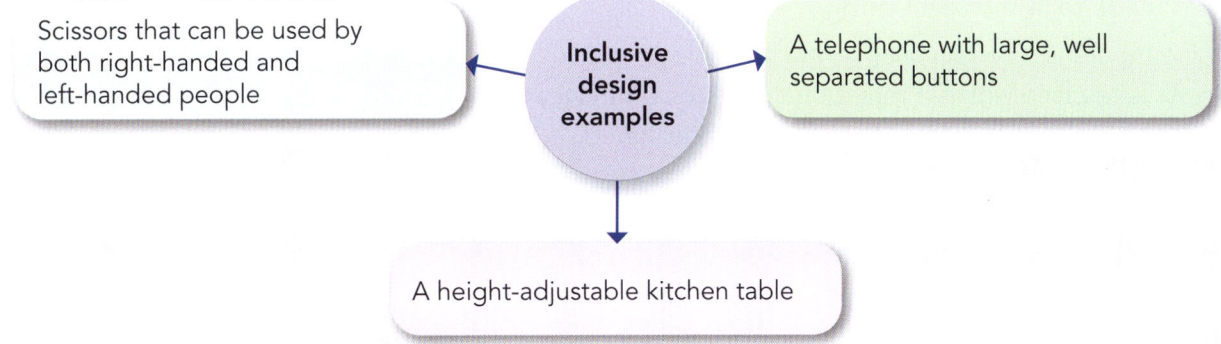

Revise it!

- Think about a person with a disability – this could be visual, physical or a learning disability.
- Make a list of the problems they may face with their daily routine and possible design solutions to those problems.

Remember it!

Inclusive design is about designing with all possible users in mind.

Revision Guide 21

Design strategies: User-centred design see p. 74

What you need to know

- What is meant by user-centred design and when it is used.
- The advantages and disadvantages of user-centred design.

When designing new products it is important that the **needs** and **wants** of the user are fully considered. **User-centred design (UCD)** is a strategy that aims to achieve this.

What is user-centred design?

A design strategy where user needs and wants are placed at the heart of the design process.

User feedback is gained at all stages.

- Often used alongside an iterative process.
- Important that the needs of the user and their individual contexts are clearly defined (for example, by producing a client/user profile).

Advantages	Disadvantages
• Ensures the product fully meets the needs of the user. • Increases user satisfaction. • Gives the user greater ownership of the design.	• Can result in a design that is too specialised towards one type of user, and therefore lacks wider commercial appeal.

When user-centred design might be used

- When users have specific requirements that must be met. For example, prosthetic limbs must be custom designed and made to fit the user's body.
- When there is a certain user context that designing must take place within. Professional athletes often wear clothing or use equipment that has been designed especially for them to improve their performance in sporting competitions.
- When looking to increase user satisfaction and sales. Successful companies such as Apple, Spotify and Duolingo focus on the needs and wants of users when designing their products.

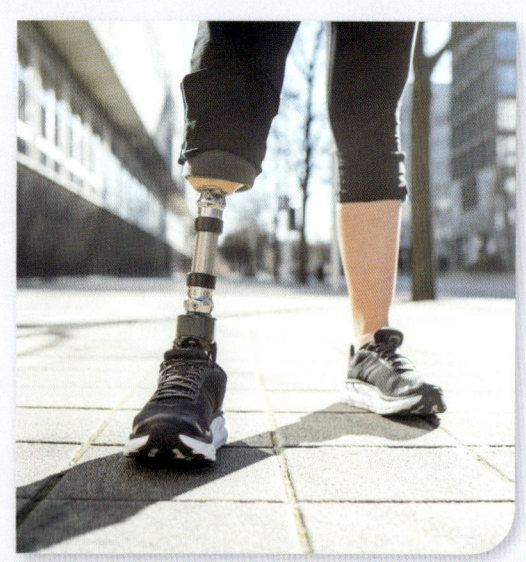

Revise it!

- Create a spider diagram with 'user-centred design' in the middle.
- Include examples of its use, and its advantages and disadvantages.

Remember it!

User-centred design is about ensuring the needs and wants of the user are considered at all stages of the design process.

Design strategies: Sustainable design see p. 74

What you need to know

- What is meant by sustainable design and how it is used.
- The advantages and disadvantages of sustainable design.

Engineers have a responsibility to ensure that their designs do not have a negative effect on the environment, and that resources can still be used by people in the future.

What is sustainable design?

Some natural resources will eventually run out; for example, oil used to make plastics and coal for power generation.

Sustainable design is about reducing the need for these resources during the design, manufacture, use and disposal of a product.

Advantages	Disadvantages
• Ensures natural resources can be used by future generations. • Reduces carbon emissions that cause global warming. • Reduces negative impacts on wildlife and natural habitats.	• Cost of replacing existing infrastructure; for example, replacing petrol fuel stations with electric charging points. • Time needed to reskill workers.

Ensuring your design is sustainable

- Make use of renewable energy sources; for example, wind, solar, hydro and biofuels.
- Make use of recycled and recyclable materials.
- Design for **longevity**, **disassembly** and **reusability**; for example, the **circular economy**.
- Apply the 6Rs of sustainability (rethink, reuse, recycle, repair, reduce, refuse).

Sustainable design examples

- Electric and hybrid vehicles.
- Water bottles made using recycled plastic.
- Solar powered lighting.
- A washing machine that is easy to disassemble.

Revise it!

Make and complete a table like the one shown here, with at least *four* sustainably designed and engineered products.

Product	How the product is sustainable	How it benefits the environment

Remember it!

Sustainable design is about ensuring that natural resources are still available to future generations.

Revision Guide

Design strategies: Ergonomic design (see p. 75)

> **What you need to know**
> - What is meant by ergonomics and how it is used when designing.
> - The advantages and disadvantages of ergonomic design.

It is important that products are comfortable to interact with and thus do not harm the user over time. **Ergonomics** is about ensuring this occurs.

What is ergonomic design?

- **Ergonomic design** is also known as human factors.
- Considers how people interact with products.
- Makes products more comfortable and safer to use.

Advantages	Disadvantages
• Individual user needs are met with regards to comfort and safety. • Reduces risk of user injuries and fatigue.	• More time needed to understand user needs when designing. • Increased costs of producing more individualised products.

Ensuring your design is ergonomic

- Consider who will use a product and how they will use it.
- Consider how easy a design will be to use or interact with, and how this could be improved.
- Make use of **anthropometric data** (**anthropometrics**) for human body sizes, shapes, etc. collected by an **anthropometrist**. This might involve **structural anthropometry** and **functional anthropometry**.

Ergonomic design examples

- A computer mouse designed to be used with the hand in a more natural, upright position to reduce discomfort and strain on the user's wrist.
- A chair with a curved shape to improve posture.
- Tools with handles that are shaped to comfortably fit the hand.
- Adjustable screens to prevent slouching when viewing them.

> **Practise it!**
> - Produce a labelled sketch of an ergonomic garden tool for use by a person with arthritis. **(3 marks)**
> - Find an example of a chair in school or at home. Suggest ways in which the ergonomics of the chair could be improved. **(2 marks)**

> **Remember it!**
> Ergonomic design is about ensuring that users can interact with products comfortably and safely.

Iterative design: Analysis of the design brief see p. 75

What you need to know
- The purpose and contents of the design brief.
- How information in the design brief contributes to the design process.

To create a successful design, engineers need to understand the problem that is to be solved. The **design brief** gives a short summary of the problem and the main user requirements.

Design brief contents

The design brief should include:
- the design context and/or situation
- the intended user and their most important needs
- a statement of the design problem
- any relevant design constraints.

It is usually written as a short paragraph.

Analysing the brief

- Engineers need to fully understand the brief so they can design a product that is fit for purpose.
- A spider diagram can be used to record early thoughts on the brief.
- It is important to discuss the brief with the user to ensure their needs are being met.

Impact of the design brief

- A clear design brief provides the foundation for the rest of the design process.
- Once the brief is fully understood a more detailed list of design criteria can be produced.
- The brief might change several times as a result of applying an iterative process.

Revise it!
Analyse an example of a design brief. What information does it contain?
Is it clear what the design problem is?
How could it be improved?

Remember it!
- The design brief is a short summary of the design problem.
- Analysing it helps the designer to understand how the problem could be solved.

Revision Guide 25

Iterative design: Methods of researching the product requirements (see p. 76)

What you need to know
- The differences between primary and secondary research.
- The sort of information that can be obtained.

As part of the iterative design process, research activities are carried out to help determine the **product requirements**.

Primary research

Research that is carried out first-hand by you. This means it is up-to-date information that is original and focused.

Can be collected through:

- surveys
- focus groups
- questionnaires
- interviews with potential users

Advantages	Disadvantages
• Current and up-to-date. • Original and detailed. • Specific to the design being researched.	• Time consuming to collect data. • Time consuming to analyse the data. • Need a large sample to get a clear view.

Secondary research

Research that is gathered from information that already exists.

Can be collected from:

- the internet
- images
- market research
- books and magazines
- data sheets and anthropometric data
- analysis of existing products using **ACCESS FM** and disassembly

Advantages	Disadvantages
• Quick to gather. • Can be from a range of sources.	• Might not be up-to-date. • Will not be specific.

Revise it!
Produce a poster to help people remember what type of research comes under each of the following headings:
- Primary research
- Secondary research

Remember it!
- **Primary research** – first-hand, up-to-date and specific.
- **Secondary research** – already exists and can be gathered from printed materials, internet and products.

Revision Guide

Iterative design: Producing an engineering design specification see p. 77

What you need to know

- How specifications are produced from the research collected.

After researching the design brief, the next step in the design cycle is to use the information to create a detailed specification.

Specification

A detailed list that gives clear and specific detail about the product being designed.

These points can often be categorised into things that *must*, *should* or *could* be included to aid the designers.

The specification points are created from the information collected during the primary and secondary research.

Will be used throughout the design cycle to compare ideas and to evaluate the final product against.

The specification includes specific points and information on the following:

 **Aesthetics**

 Cost

 Customer

 Environment

 Size

 Safety

 Function

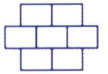 Materials

Practise it!

Write down *four* points that the designer would have had to work towards for this product. **(4 marks)**

Remember it!

Specification = ACCESS FM

- Aesthetics
- Cost
- Customer
- Environment
- Size
- Safety
- Function
- Materials

Revision Guide

Iterative design: Generating design ideas by sketching and modelling see p. 77

What you need to know

- How the research and specification help guide the design ideas.

Once the research has been carried out and the specification listed, the next step is to produce design ideas.

Design ideas

The design phase of the process involves producing a range of initial design ideas, not just one idea.

These could be sketches of the whole product or part of it, or modifications to products that already exist.

Designers may use modelling to help generate ideas.

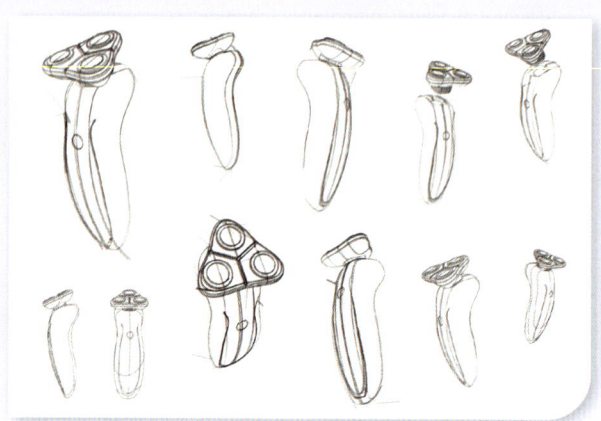

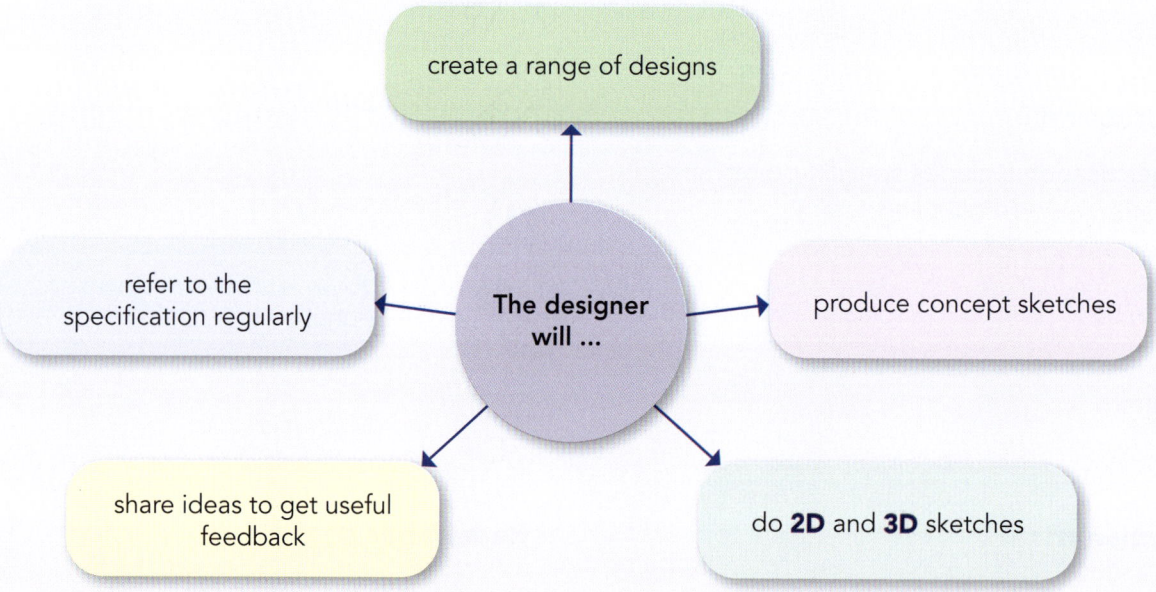

Revise it!

Sketch *four* improved designs for a television remote control to fit the following specification requirements:

- Must have easy grip for people with mobility issues.
- Must have clear, easy-to-read buttons.

Remember it!

Design – a range of sketches that fit the specification points produced from the results of the research.

Iterative design: Reasons for using modelling see p. 78

What you need to know

- Why it is important for designers to use the modelling stage of the design process.

As part of the design process, modelling is used to help the designer progress with their idea development.

Modelling

Whether designing a full new product or making modifications to an existing one, modelling is very important to allow the designer to see and check:

- size, scale and proportions
- aesthetics
- ergonomics
- function.

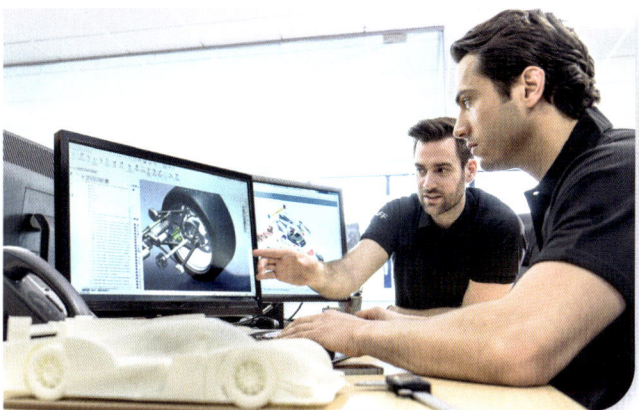

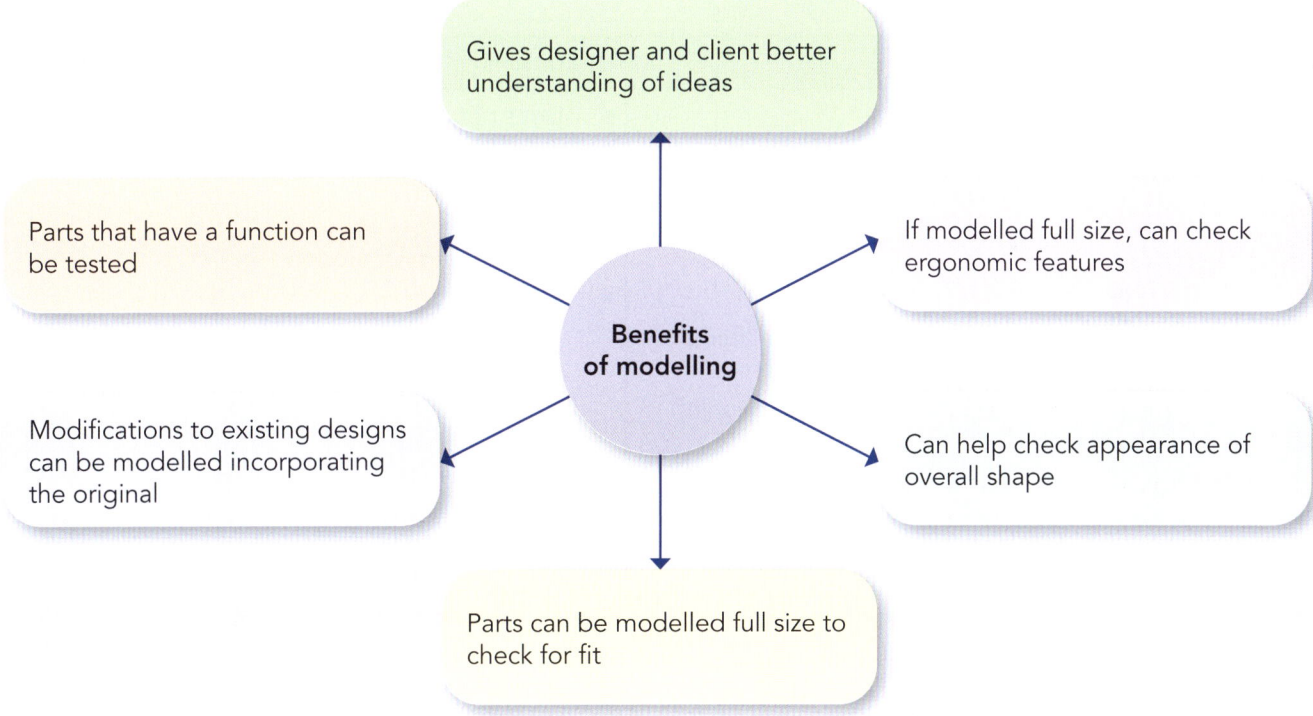

Revise it!

Produce a mind map of all the things that a designer would gain from modelling a new camping chair design.

Remember it!

Modelling allows designers to test:

- proportions
- scale
- function.

Revision Guide

Iterative design: Virtual modelling of design ideas   see p. 78

What you need to know

- Why virtual modelling is important to the design process.

Designers can use several modelling techniques to help visualise and test design ideas. Some require hands-on modelling skills and others require computer skills.

Virtual modelling

Virtual modelling is done using **computer aided design (CAD)** packages that allow the idea to be modelled on screen in 3D.

Using a visual model on screen, the design can be checked against the specification and design brief.

Virtual modelling will require a skilled user of the CAD package being used.

Benefits	Limitations
- Allows product to be seen in 3D. - Can be quickly edited. - Can be rendered to look like the intended materials. - Can be tested on screen for things like movement (if it has moving parts), weight and stress on the materials. - Does not require physical equipment and materials to make the model, which saves time and money. - Allows the design to be easily shared with people all over the globe. - Can be tested within a virtual environment. - Design once correct can be used for **computer aided manufacture (CAM)**.	- Does not allow you to do hands-on testing. - Does not allow you to check the physical size of the product. - Does not allow you to check if a new part fits with the original product. - Complexity of model is limited by the skill of the CAD operator.

Revise it!

Produce a mind map showing how a virtual model could benefit both the client and the designer.

Remember it!

Virtual modelling allows a range of on-screen testing.

Iterative design: Physical modelling (see p. 78)

What you need to know
- How physical modelling aids the designer.

As part of the design process, physical models are used to demonstrate all or part of a design.

Physical modelling

Physical modelling can be carried out using a range of materials including card, clay, wood and additive manufacturing (3D printing). Electronic circuit ideas can also be modelled on a breadboard.

By having a physical **model**, the designer can gain information about modifications that need to be made to the design.

Benefits	Limitations
• Allows for a model that can be touched and held. • Can be tested by the intended user. • For designs with different parts, fit and function of them can be checked. • Shape and ergonomics can be tested. • Can be full size or to scale.	• Not normally modelled in the material that the final design will be made from. • For 3D-printed models, a CAD file will be needed. • Not easy to modify and often need remaking.

When physical modelling might be used

Designers use physical models so they can touch, see and test their design. For example, some car models are built in clay before production. This shows how light interacts with the curves of the vehicle, and also allows them to be tested in wind tunnels for aerodynamics.

Practise it!

What type of modelling could be best for the following design ideas? Explain your reasons for selection.

- Eco-friendly packaging for posting out products. **(2 marks)**
- A handle grip for a kettle for the elderly. **(2 marks)**

Remember it!

Physical modelling allows you to:
- touch
- see
- test.

Revision Guide 31

Iterative design: Manufacturing or modifying a prototype

see p. 78

What you need to know

- The next step in the design cycle when the testing has been carried out.

There is no point in modelling and testing a design if the findings of the test and checks against the specification are not followed up.

Comparison against design brief and specification

All designs need to be compared with the design brief and the specification to check that the design meets the requirements.

If a design is found to fully meet all the requirements of the design brief and specification, it can then progress to the manufacturing stage.

If a design does not fully meet the requirements, it will need to be modified.

Modifications

- If modifications are picked up during the design stage, can save money and time
- Can be time consuming depending on modelling method
- Help make sure that the design is fully fit for purpose
- If big changes, a new model might need to be made and tested

Practise it!

- Which modelling process allows for the quickest modifications? **(1 mark)**
- Which modelling process allows hands-on testing but will take longer to modify if needed? **(1 mark)**

Remember it!

- Check against design brief and specification.
- Modifications make sure that the design fully meets the requirements.

Design criteria: Needs and wants see p. 79

What you need to know
- What a design specification is.
- The difference between needs and wants.

Once a design brief has been set and the research has been carried out, the information is used to develop the design criteria; this is called the **design specification**.

Design specification

The design specification states the key design requirements needed to meet the brief. This information is found from the research. It is normally written as a list and contains specific, detailed facts.

Included in a specification are:
- needs and wants
- quantitative and qualitative criteria
- ACCESS FM.

Needs

'Needs' are what the product must do or have to function as intended.

For a smartphone, the needs could include:
- make calls (the main purpose of a phone is to make calls)
- send texts (a function most people use daily)
- have a clear signal (without this, the phone is of no use).

Wants

'Wants' are what the users would like, but are not necessary for the product to function as intended.

For a smartphone, the wants could include:
- available in a range of colours (this won't affect the product's function, but might appeal to a broader customer range)
- have a high-quality camera (this won't affect making calls or sending texts, but means the user doesn't need a separate camera).

Revise it!
Imagine you are set the brief to design a new games console. Make a list of:
- the key information you need to know from your design specification
- the users' possible needs and wants.

Remember it!
- Specification – criteria you design to.
- Needs – essential requirements.
- Wants – users' preferences.

Revision Guide

Design criteria: Quantitative and qualitative see p. 80

What you need to know
- The difference between quantitative and qualitative criteria.
- How and why these criteria are used in design specifications.

Quantitative and qualitative criteria are found during research into the design brief, and are used in specifications.

Quantitative research

Criteria that are:
- measurable
- counted
- expressed as numbers.

Examples: length, width, cost, time

Quantitative criteria are **objective** which means they are factual, numerical and not influenced by personal feelings or opinions.

Qualitative research

Criteria that are:
- descriptions
- characteristics
- observations.

Examples: colours, textures, appearance

Qualitative criteria are **subjective**: judged based on the opinion of the assessor. Qualitative research may involve market research to establish the opinion of the majority of users.

Practise it!
For a product of your choice, write down *three* quantitative and *three* qualitative specification criteria. **(6 marks)**

Remember it!
Quantitative: Quantity – can be expressed as a number.
Qualitative: Quality – descriptive point.

34 Revision Guide

Design criteria: ACCESS FM   see p. 81

What you need to know

- ACCESS FM and what it stands for.
- Why these criteria are important and why they need to be included in specifications.

The design specification is made up of key points and facts that must be met. These points cover key areas, which can be remembered using the mnemonic ACCESS FM.

Criteria and reasons for including

A	Aesthetics	Key features about how the product should look.
C	Cost	The product will need to be manufactured at a cost that allows it to be marketed within a specific price range.
C	Customer	The product must be designed with the customer in mind; for example, think about age range and gender.
E	Environment	How is the product going to affect the environment? Will it cause pollution or waste?
S	Size	The design will need set size constraints.
S	Safety	Key features that will make the product safe for the user.
F	Function	A clear description of what the product is intended to do.
M	Materials	Clear statements of what can and can't be used in the product.

ACCESS FM example questions

Aesthetics – Does the product look good? How does it use colour?

Cost – How much will it cost to make the product? What price can you sell it for?

Customer – Who is the product for? Where would they use it?

Environment – How long will it last? Can it be recycled?

Size – Are the proportions appropriate for its function?

Safety – Have any safety concerns been thought about in the design?

Function – Does the product work? How easy is it to use?

Materials – What kind of material has been used? Would another material have worked better?

Revise it!

You are a designer working on a new floor-mounted television stand.

For each ACCESS FM criterion:

- write down a clear specification point
- explain why that information should be included.

Remember it!

- ACCESS FM gives designers clear constraints to design to.
- Includes criteria to be included and things to avoid.

Revision Guide

Manufacturing considerations: Scale (see p. 81)

What you need to know
- How manufacturing considerations affect design.
- The four main areas that need to be considered.

When designing new products, the designer must consider anything that might affect production.

Scale of manufacture

The quantity of the product required determines the **manufacturing processes** and materials used to manufacture it.

Scale of manufacture affects the overall cost of manufacturing and, therefore, the profits made by the company.

Companies will be more willing to spend on new equipment and processes if they are making a larger quantity.

Manufacture can be **one-off production**, **batch production** or **mass production**.

One-off
- Often more hand processes used in manufacture.
- High quality but at higher cost.
- Bespoke (made to customers' individual requirements).

Examples: handmade furniture, high performance cars, bridges and stadiums.

Batch
- Produced in set quantities.
- Parts for mass produced products.
- Lower **production costs**.
- Good for seasonal products.

Examples: circuit boards, clothes, flatpack furniture and jet engines.

Mass
- Continuous production of large number of identical items.
- Automated manufacture.
- Lower production costs.
- Faster production rates.

Examples: canned food, household appliances, nuts and bolts.

Revise it!
Create a table of advantages and disadvantages of the different scales of production.

Remember it!
- One-off – made one at a time.
- Batch – specific amount made.
- Mass – large quantity made.

Manufacturing considerations: Availability and form see p. 82

What you need to know
- How material availability can affect designs.
- Why designers need to know about material forms.

When designing a new product, the designer needs to think about what materials to use and what form they are available in. They must also think about suitability and material properties.

Material availability

Availability of a material is important when designing a new product.

The designer must ask themselves:
- is it readily available?
- will it continue to be available over the period of production time for the product?

Failure to think about availability could lead to:
- lost money and time if the product has been fully designed and developed, but the required materials are not available
- delay in manufacturing if the material needs to be changed or sourced from elsewhere.

Material form

Materials are available in standard shapes, forms and colours. This makes ordering and supply for manufacturing simpler.

Metal examples: plates, sheets, rods, bars, tubes

Wood examples: dowels, planks, sheets

Polymer examples: pellets, powdered mix

If a premanufactured form can be used without a lot of modification then money can be saved on the processing stage.

Revise it!
Imagine you are set the brief to design a new computer monitor. Create a mind map to help you decide what materials you would require, and what stock forms you would need to be ready for manufacture.

Remember it!
- Readily available materials.
- Stock forms – standard sizes and shapes.
- Save production time and money.

Revision Guide

Manufacturing considerations: Processes *see p. 82*

What you need to know

- The different types of manufacturing processes.
- How these might affect the design.

The designer must think about the processes that will be used to make the product. These could be existing processes that are available to them, or they may need to factor in the cost of developing new processes.

Processes

Process	Description	Examples
Wasting	Removing excess material by cutting away with tools and equipment.	chiselling, filing, sanding
Shaping	Changing the state or shape.	casting, moulding, 3D printing
Forming	Using heat and/or force to form the material into a different shape.	vacuum forming, pressing, forging
Joining	Fixing parts of the product together to form more complex parts.	gluing, welding, riveting, soldering
Finishing	Adding a protective and/or decorative layer to the surface of the product.	painting, varnishing, power coating, polishing
Assembly	Fitting parts together to make the final product.	using screws, bolts, clips

Practise it!

Select *two* products from this photograph.

List *three* processes that will have been used to make each one. **(6 marks)**

Remember it!

The more processes there are, the higher the cost to manufacture.

- Remove the waste.
- Shape and/or form the parts.
- Join parts together to form more complex parts.
- Add a finish if needed.
- Assemble the parts to complete the item.

Manufacturing considerations: Production costs see p. 83

What you need to know

- How designers must take production costs into account when designing.
- What labour and capital costs are.

When designing a new product, the designer needs to think about overall production costs so they design a product that is within the set budget.

Production costs

It is important to consider **production costs** when designing new products.

These costs need to be totalled up and divided by the number of products being made. This will allow the customer to see if the project is cost effective. New products need to be cost effective to make them viable.

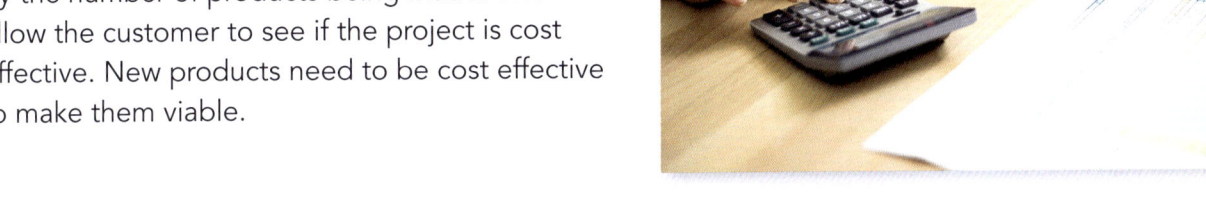

Labour costs

Labour costs, the costs of paying for people to make the product, can be greatly affected by the design of the product.

- Many parts to fit together.
- Specialist skills needed.
- Not an automated system.

These are long term costs that are needed throughout the whole period of manufacture – they are ongoing.

Capital costs

Capital costs are the initial costs of setting up the manufacturing facility to make the new product.

- Purchasing new manufacturing space.
- Material costs (does it have to be that type of material or could a cheaper one be used?)
- Tooling and machinery costs (what new tools are needed? Which ones, long term, will need to be replaced?)

These one-off costs need to be recovered over a planned period of time.

Revise it!

Imagine you have been tasked with setting up a new factory to produce injection moulded phone cases.

Create an information page that answers:

- what expenditures would come under capital costs?
- will the production costs vary for each batch?
- will there be high or low labour costs?

Remember it!

- Capital costs – initial set up of facility.
- Production costs – overall cost of making the product.
- Labour costs – long term while the production is happening.

Revision Guide

Influences on product design: Pull and push see p. 83

What you need to know

- What influences a product's design.
- How these factors change a product.

When designing a new product, designers have to think about certain factors that will influence its design, style and function.

Influencing the design

Many factors can influence the design of a new product. The main ones are:

- **market pull** and **technology push**
- British and international standards
- **legislation**
- **planned obsolescence**
- sustainable design
- designing for the circular economy.

Market pull

Market pull is when consumer demand causes the need for a new product. It can happen when research shows a need for a product to solve a common problem.

An example of market pull is the development of digital cameras. Users wanted to take as many photos as they liked and view them immediately, but the film in old-style cameras limited the number of photos and took time to develop. To meet consumer demand, manufacturers invested time, money and research into developing the required technology.

Technology push

Technology push is when new products are 'pushed' onto the market as a result of research and development being carried out. There is not necessarily a demand for the product.

An example of technology push is the development of touchscreens. Finger-touch display was first invented in the 1960s, but was not very reliable to begin with. Thanks to research and investment, the technology was gradually refined and manufacturers started to use it in products. Nowadays, it is difficult to imagine phones, tablets, computers, watches and even cars without their touchscreens!

Practise it!

A new phone comes onto the market with an upgraded screen and processor – is this market pull or technology push?

Explain your answer in terms of customers and technology development. **(3 marks)**

Remember it!

- Market pull – consumer demand.
- Technology push – development of new technology.

40 Revision Guide

Influences on product design: Standards *see p. 84*

What you need to know

- What British Standards are and how they influence designs.
- What international standards are and how they influence designs.

When designers design new products, they must make sure that they meet certain standards, otherwise they will be classed as unsafe and unmarketable.

British Standards

British Standards are produced by the British Standards Institution (BSI). Products must meet a range of quality checks through testing to become certified to these standards. Certain products that are found to meet criteria for quality and accuracy can bear the BSI Kitemark logo.

CE

The CE marking is required on products sold in the European Union (EU). The mark indicates that the product has been assessed to meet the high safety, health and environmental protection requirements of the EU.

UKCA

United Kingdom Conformity Assessed (UKCA) is the new UK marking that has replaced the CE marking, and goes on products marketed in England, Scotland and Wales.

The UKCA mark, like the CE mark, indicates that the product conforms to the required standards.

International Standards

International Standards are created by the International Organization for Standardization (ISO). They develop standards to make sure that products are good quality, safe and efficient.

Some products have to comply with British Standards and some have to comply with both British Standards and ISO standards.

Practise it!

- State *two* qualities that products must have in order to meet the British Standards. **(2 marks)**
- State the reasons for ISO standards. **(2 marks)**
- Draw the UKCA logo. **(1 mark)**

Remember it!

- **BSI** – British Standards Institution
- **ISO** – International Organization for Standardization
- **UKCA** – United Kingdom Conformity Assessed

Influences on product design: Legislation (see p. 85)

What you need to know

- What legislation is.

When designing products, the designers have to make sure that the product will comply with legislation.

What is legislation?

Legislation is laws that have been proposed by the government and then passed as Acts of Parliament.

A company or individual can be **prosecuted** and fined or jailed if they break a law.

Products must be designed and manufactured to comply with standards listed in the legislation.

Legislation is designed to protect the consumer or user of a product.

Health and Safety at Work

The Health and Safety at Work Act (HASAWA):
- lists duties that the employer and employee must follow
- ensures that the workplace is a safe place to work.

All products designed need to be manufactured within these rules. They also need to operate in a way that allows the employer and employees to be safe.

Risk assessments

Risk assessments identify risks and give guidance on how to reduce the risk of an accident happening.

When designing a product, the designer needs to make sure that the product will be safe to use for its intended purpose.

They also need to make sure that it reduces the chance of others being injured through misuse.

Practise it!

These two products have been designed to meet legislation that protects the users.

List *three* safety features and what accidents they are designed to avoid. **(3 marks)**

Remember it!

Legislation:
- a set of laws that, if broken, will get you into trouble
- written to protect the manufacturers and the consumers.

HASAWA – Health and Safety at Work Act.

Risk assessments – identify risk and ways to stop accidents happening.

Influences on product design: Planned obsolescence *see p. 86*

What you need to know

- What planned obsolescence is.
- How this influences the design of products.

Planned obsolescence can influence the design of products and the materials used to make them.

Obsolescence

Obsolescence is:

- uselessness
- undesirability.

Some products become obsolete because of the changing times and user's wants. Others become obsolete because they fail to continue to do the job they were intended for.

Planned obsolescence

When a product fails and needs replacing within a relatively short time, it is often planned to happen by the designer.

- Forces people to replace the product.
- Products often designed to make replacement more cost effective than repair.
- Bad for the environment.

Example: Technology companies will stop issuing system updates for a smartphone model after a set period of time, which means users cannot access certain features and their phones are more vulnerable to bugs. This encourages the user to replace their device.

Practise it!

- State *three* advantages of planned obsolescence that benefit the designers, manufacturers and consumers. **(3 marks)**
- State *three* disadvantages of planned obsolescence. **(3 marks)**

Remember it!

Planned obsolescence:

- is when something is designed to fail after a certain time
- forces the consumer to replace the item.

Revision Guide 43

Influences on product design: Sustainable design and the circular economy see p. 87

What you need to know

- What sustainable design is.
- What the 6Rs that are used to explain sustainable design are.

Sustainable design is about long-term thinking and making products better for the environment. It is often discussed in terms of the 6Rs.

Sustainable design

The 6Rs

RETHINK — Can you design the product with a different material?

RECYCLE — Can the materials be recycled? Will the product be easy to separate into the base materials to recycle them?

REDUCE — Is the product durable so that it will be long lasting and not need replacing regularly?

REUSE — Can the product be reused for the same purpose or another to extend its life?

REPAIR — If the product breaks can it be easily repaired? Will this be cost effective to the user?

REFUSE — Can you refuse to use materials or processes in the design that are not sustainable?

The circular economy

An ongoing cycle to reduce the use of raw materials by recycling existing materials for as long as possible.

- Produce the product.
- Use the product.
- Recycle the materials.
- Make another product.
- Use the new product.
- Recycle the materials.
- Make another product.

Revise it!

Create a mind map showing why it is important to design new products with sustainability in mind. Include information about why designing products that can fit with a circular economy is going to benefit the environment.

Remember it!

- 6Rs – rethink, reuse, recycle, repair, reduce, refuse.
- Circular economy – produce, use, recycle, repeat.

Revision Guide

Types of drawing: Freehand and isometric (see p. 88)

What you need to know

- Different types of drawings used in engineering.
- The applications, advantages and disadvantages of each type.

Different types of drawing styles allow designs to be shown in different ways. Some have more accurate detail than others.

Freehand

A **sketch** of an idea without using a ruler. Used to visualise initial ideas.

Advantages
• Quick way of sharing an idea. • No special equipment needed.
Disadvantages
• May not be accurate. • Needs developing with more detail to allow product to be made.

Isometric

A drawing that shows a product in three dimensions. Drawn with two lines at a 30° angle from the centre line.

Advantages
• Shows the product in 3D with three sides on display. • Can be drawn to accurate measurements.
Disadvantages
• Needs a 30/60 set square to draw accurately. • Needs more than one drawing to show all sides in detail.

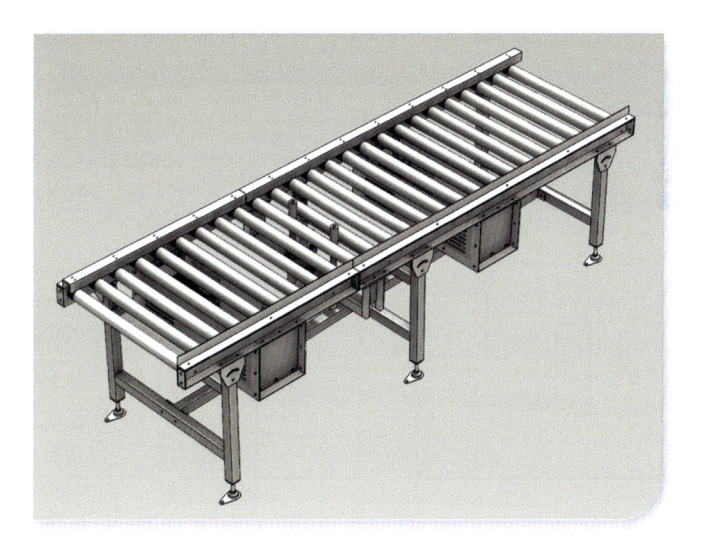

Revise it!

Produce an isometric sketch of your phone. Remember to start with a centre line and then two lines coming off at 30° to each side.

Remember it!

- **Freehand sketching**: quick; no special equipment needed; not accurate
- **Isometric drawing**: 3D; accurate sizes; 30° angle

Revision Guide

Types of drawing: Oblique and orthographic (see p. 88)

What you need to know

- Different types of drawings used in engineering.
- The applications of each type of drawing.

Designs sometimes need to be in 3D and sometimes in 2D with accurate measurements.

Oblique

A drawing using lines at a 45° angle.

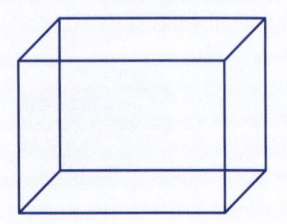

Advantages
• Shows a shape in 3D, with clear 2D details of front face.
• Easy to draw with limited equipment.
Disadvantages
• Not very realistic.
• Needs developing with more detail to allow product to be made.

There are two main types of oblique drawing. In **cavalier oblique** the lines are drawn to actual measurements, so the design is accurate but the drawing looks stretched. In **cabinet oblique** the lines showing depth are made shorter, which means the design is less accurate but the drawing looks more like the intended object.

Orthographic

A drawing that shows a 2D view without any perspective. The drawing can include views of more than one side, as projections. For more on orthographic projections, see page 50.

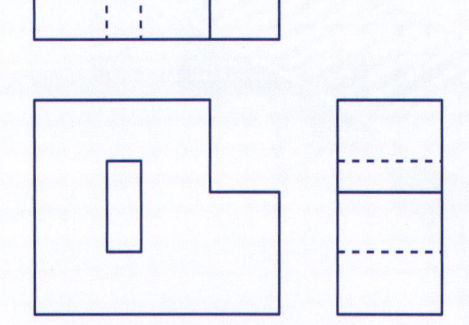

Advantages
• Shows clear details including hidden detail.
• Used to help manufacturers plan production.
• Has dimensions needed for manufacture.
Disadvantages
• Needs time and skill to produce.
• Needs to be paired with a 3D view to help visualise complex items.

Practise it!

- Draw a television in cavalier oblique. **(2 marks)**
- What detail can you not see in just one drawing? **(1 mark)**
- What extra detail could you see if you had drawn an orthographic drawing instead? **(2 marks)**

Remember it!

Oblique drawing
- 45° angle.
- Shows limited detail.

Orthographic drawing
- Shows three views.
- Can include clear measurements.
- Manufacturers use this.

Types of drawing:
Exploded views and assembly drawings see p. 88

What you need to know

- Different types of drawings used in engineering.
- The applications of each type of drawing.

Once manufacturers have made all the individual parts of a product, they need to know how they fit together.

Exploded view

A detailed drawing that shows how the parts of a product fit together.

Advantages
• Helps engineers to understand the assembly order. • Allows hidden parts to be shown.
Disadvantages
• Is complex and time consuming to produce. • Does not show the finished assembled item.

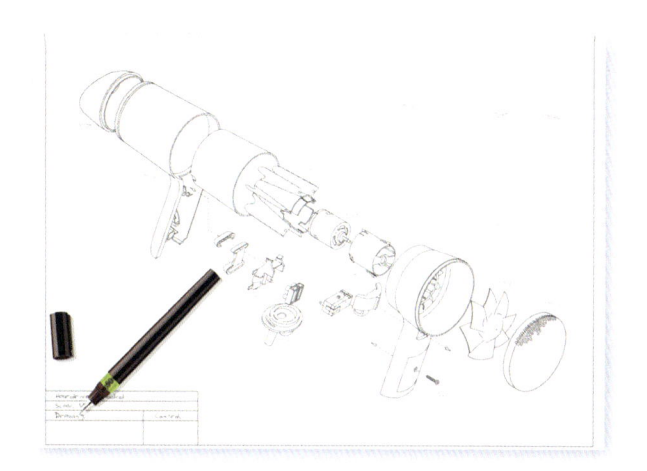

Assembly drawing

A drawing showing how individual parts are fitted together.

Advantages
• Shows how items with more than one part fit together. • Helps reduce the number of products that are assembled incorrectly.
Disadvantages
• More than one drawing will be needed for complex items. • Does not show measurements.

Revise it!

Study a product that you can see.

How many individual parts do you think have been used to make it? Include small items such as screws, nuts and bolts.

Remember it!

- **Exploded view** – product is exploded apart on the page showing how it all fits together.
- **Assembly drawing** – shows how separate components fit together.

Revision Guide

Types of drawing: Block diagrams and flowcharts (see p. 88)

What you need to know
- Different types of drawings used in engineering.
- The applications of each type of drawing.

Engineering design can also involve electronics. **Block diagrams** and flowcharts help designers to analyse systems before they design the actual circuit.

Block diagrams
Key parts of a system shown as boxes linked with arrows.

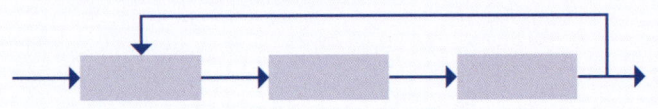

Can be split into inputs, processes, outputs and feedback loops.

Advantages
• Easy way to visualise how a system works. • Easy to draw.
Disadvantages
• Only gives basic information. • Does not give construction details.

Flowcharts
A diagram that represents a process.

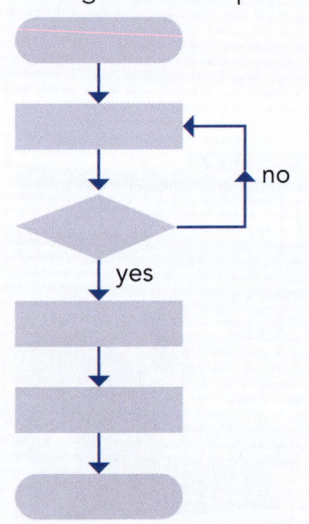

Starts or ends flowchart.	⬭
Decisions can be made with 'yes' and 'no' loops.	◇
Processes that need to happen.	▭

Advantages
• Easy way to represent a process. • Can show where decisions need to be made.
Disadvantages
• Will become large for a complex process. • Hard to edit without redrawing the whole process.

Revise it!
Draw a block diagram for the process needed to make a kettle boil.

Draw a flowchart for the process needed to make a sandwich; include at least one decision.

To check if you have the processes correct, ask someone else to try to identify or follow the process without telling them what it is. Can they follow it successfully?

Remember it!
- Block diagram – easy to draw to show basic systems.
- Flowcharts – allow more detailed processes to be drawn.

48 Revision Guide

Types of drawing:
Circuit diagrams and wiring diagrams see p. 88

What you need to know

- Different types of drawings used in engineering.
- The applications of each type of drawing.

Circuit diagrams and wiring diagrams are very important to show how components are connected together.

Circuit diagrams

A way of showing how individual components are connected in a circuit.

Advantages
• Clearly shows how the components are fitted together.
• Standard symbols are used.

Disadvantages
• Hard to read if you do not understand the circuit symbols.
• Slow to draw manually without CAD software.

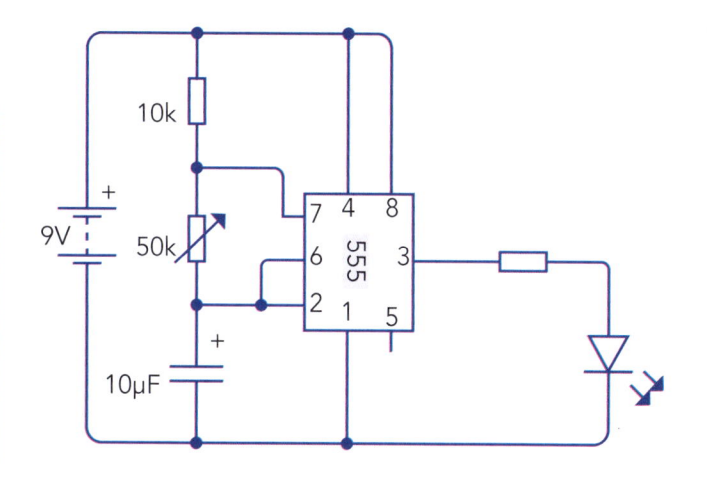

Wiring diagrams

A simplified pictorial diagram of a circuit.

Used to show how components of an electronic product are wired together.

Advantages
• Clearly shows connections between parts.
• Simplified diagrams of components are easier to read.
• Gives information about relative positions of parts.

Disadvantages
• Hard to read if you don't know what the diagrams are representing.

Revise it!

Make a spider diagram to show the key information that you can gain from reading a wiring diagram.

Make a list of the information that you can record on a circuit diagram using standard symbols.

Remember it!

Circuit diagram – uses standard symbols to show how components are connected in a circuit.

Wiring diagram – shows how parts of a circuit are connected together.

Revision Guide 49

Working drawings:
Third angle orthographic projection *see p. 90*

What you need to know

- Why working drawings are important.
- What information is included on a working drawing.

Working drawings provide technical information required by manufacturers to make a product. Each part will have its own drawing.

Third angle orthographic projection

A **third angle orthographic projection** is used to show three different views of a part, product or design in 2D (front, plan and side). Projections are drawn on the same diagram and are aligned so that the relationship between them is clear to see. They show detailed information, such as dimensions and hidden details. Manufacturers use projections to make parts.

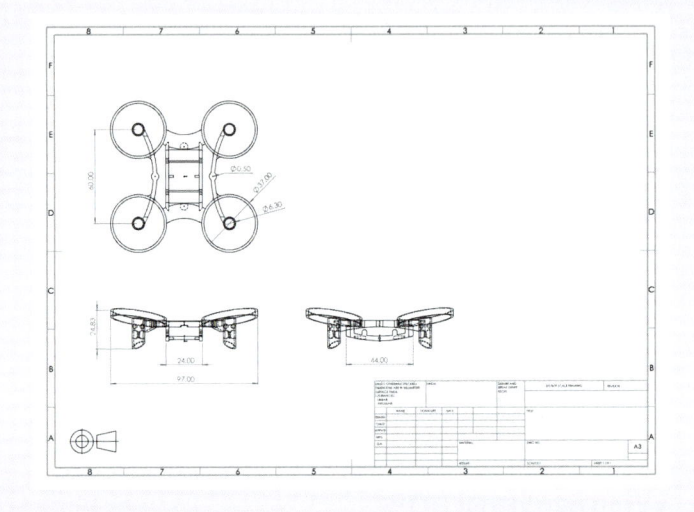

This symbol is included in the title block of third angle orthographic projection drawings.

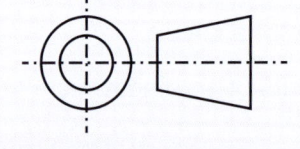

Revise it!

Draw a third angle orthographic projection for this part.

You do not need to draw to scale.

Remember it!

Third angle orthographic projections show three views of the same part.
- Plan
- Side
- Front

50 Revision Guide

Working drawings: Standard conventions *(see p. 90)*

What you need to know

- What the standard conventions on a working drawing are.
- Why each one is used.

Working drawings must follow **standard conventions** so that any engineer can read the diagram and work from it without the risk of error from misreading it.

Title block

Contains important information about the drawing or part.

- Part name.
- Drawing number (so you can quickly tell if a complex part has more than one drawing).
- Scale.
- Tolerance.
- Materials and finishes.

Scale

If a scale is given on the drawing it means that the drawing is accurate and measurements can be taken directly off the picture.

Parts might be too big to draw full size on a sheet, so they are scaled; the scale is given on the drawing.

If the drawing says 'Do Not Scale' it means that measurements cannot be gained by measuring the picture as it is not accurate.

Metric units

Drawing measurements are usually in millimetres.

- Allows for consistency across parts on different drawings.
- Accurate.
- Easy to read.
- Only need one set of measuring equipment at the manufacturing stage.

Tolerance

Tolerance states the maximum and minimum dimensions for a part that will allow it to fit and work as intended.

For example, symmetrical tolerance is written as:

± 0.25

This would mean a part that is 50 mm long can be a minimum of 49.75 mm long and a maximum of 50.25 mm long.

Asymmetrical tolerance is written as:

$$20 \begin{array}{c} +0.5 \\ -0.6 \end{array} \quad \text{or} \quad \begin{array}{c} 19.4 \\ 20.5 \end{array}$$

Revise it!

A part is drawn to a scale of 2 : 1.
One of the lines represents a 50 mm length. How long is this line on the drawing?
(Try drawing the line yourself.)

A part must be made to 26 mm **diameter** with a tolerance of 0.15 mm. What are the maximum and minimum sizes of the part?

Remember it!

Title block – holds key information about the part. Measurements are normally in metric.

Scale – drawings often state they are not drawn to scale; in this case, do not measure off them.

Tolerance – how much over or under the stated size the part can be and still work.

Revision Guide

Working drawings: Dimensions (see p. 91)

What you need to know

- What the standard conventions for measurements are on a working drawing.

When adding measurements to a drawing, standard conventions should be followed so that the measurements are clear and consistent across different diagrams.

Linear measurements

Linear measurements should always be recorded with lines and arrows so it is clear where they are measuring.

Diameter

This dimension is shown as a number with Ø in front of the number.

There is then an arrow pointing to the outside of the circle that the dimension refers to.

Radius

The **radius** is written with a capital R before the number and an arrow pointing from the number to the curved part.

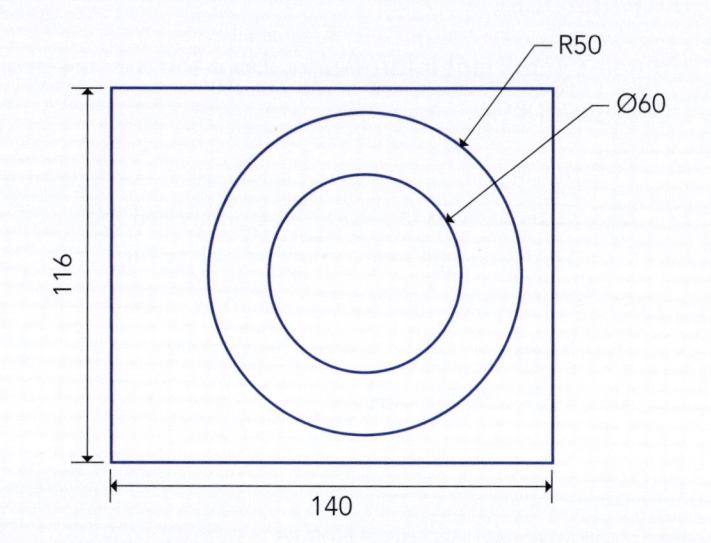

Surface finish

The **surface finish** can affect whether a part will work successfully, so it is as important as stating the measurements.

It is important for manufacturing engineers to know which type of **machined finish** a product should have.

Practise it!

- What measurement is the 'radius' of a circle? **(1 mark)**
- What measurement is the 'diameter' of a circle, and what symbol is used to represent it? **(2 marks)**
- Do you need to add radius and diameter to a single drawing of a circle? Explain your answer. **(2 marks)**

Remember it!

R = Radius
Ø = Diameter

Dimensions are in mm and need to have arrows on both ends and a fine line showing where the measurement starts and stops.

Working drawings: Line types see p. 91

What you need to know

- What each of the different line types represent.

Different line types are used to share different information on diagrams. Standard ones are used so that detail can be shared visually without the need for extra labels.

Outlines

A thick line is used for the outside edge of the part.

Hidden detail

A dashed line is used to show detail that is hidden behind the visible surface.

Centre line

A line of long and short dashes is used to show where the centre is on a part.

Projection

A thin line is used to show how one drawing view links to other views.

Dimension

A medium line with solid arrowheads on each end is used to show distances on the drawing.

Leader line

A thin line drawn at an angle with an arrow on the end is used to show a link from a piece of information to a specific point on a drawing.

Revise it!

Practise producing all the different types of lines using just a pencil and ruler.

Don't press too hard, unless you are trying to do the outline.

Try drawing an oblique cube that is 80 mm square, with a 40 mm diameter hole through. Use the correct lines to show the details.

Remember it!

- **Thick** – outlines.
- **Thin** – projection lines.
- **Dimensions** – must have arrows.
- **Leader line** – points to where it needs you to look.

Revision Guide

Working drawings: Mechanical features *see p. 91*

What you need to know

- How different mechanical features are represented in engineering drawings.

Mechanical features are displayed on drawings in a graphical method so they are easy to identify.

External threads

An external thread is a thread cut into the outside of the part. This is so it can be screwed into something.

In technical drawing, the depth of the thread is shown as two parallel lines on the side view. One set of lines represents the widest part of the thread and a second set of lines represents the narrowest. On the front view, this is shown by a complete circle for the widest and an incomplete circle for the narrowest.

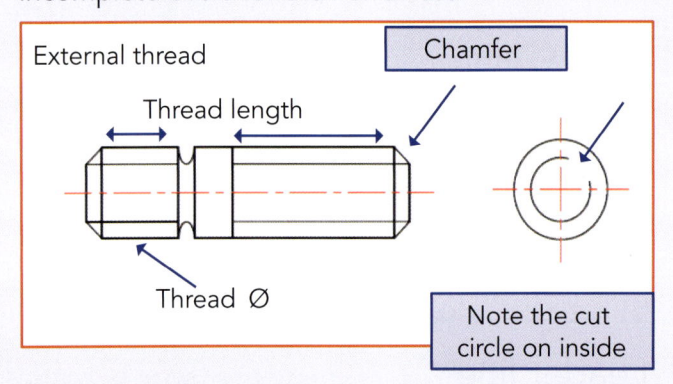

Internal threads

An internal thread is a thread cut into the inside of the part. This is so something can be screwed into it.

In technical drawing, the two parallel lines showing the depth are represented by hidden lines. On the front view, this is shown by an incomplete circle for the outside diameter.

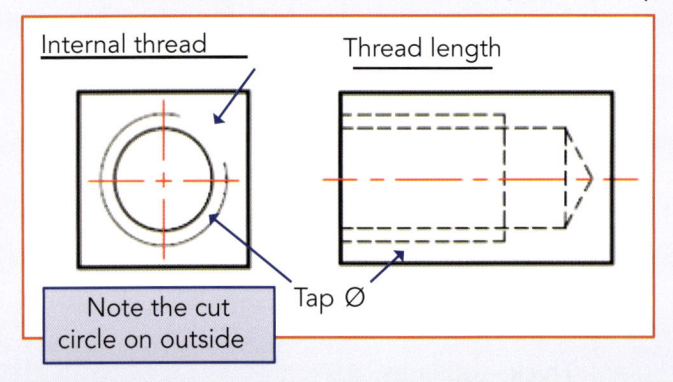

Chamfers

A chamfer is a sloping edge cut into the corner of two sides. This is done to remove sharp edges, which protects other parts and makes the product safer for the user.

Countersinks

A countersink is a well that allows a bolt or screw head to fit flush against the surface. This is so it doesn't stick out of the material. The countersink is added around the top of a hole before a product is assembled. In technical drawing, the angle of one edge of the hole to another is added above the countersink and the centre line shows the centre of the hole.

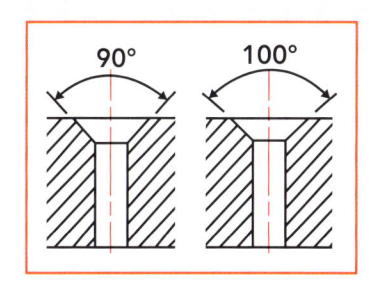

Holes

A hole is a connection point for screws, bolts or other components to fit into. A blind hole is made to a specified depth without breaking through to the other side of the material. A through hole goes completely through the material from one side to another.

In technical drawing, the dotted lines indicate the width and depth of the hole and the centre line shows the centre of the hole.

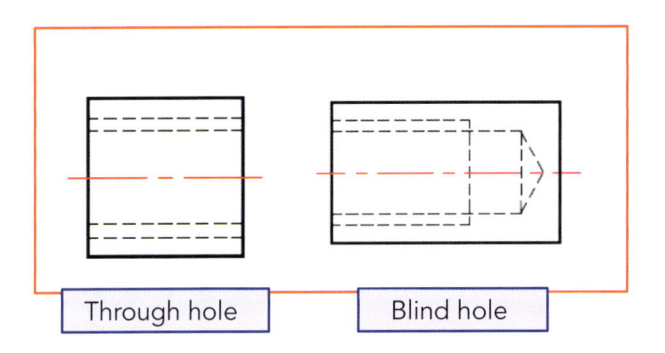

Through hole

Blind hole

Knurls

A knurl is a texture added to a material to add grip. This is so the user can more easily hold, lift or turn the part.

In technical drawing, knurling can be represented by a pattern of parallel lines (straight knurling) or crossed lines (diamond knurling). Note that the knurl doesn't fill the entire area and is drawn using much thinner lines to the outlines.

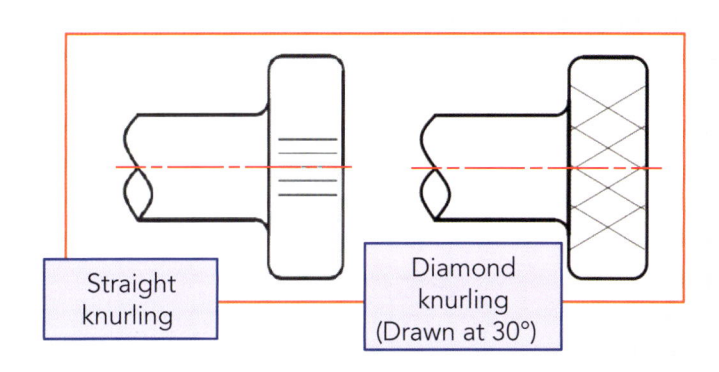

Straight knurling

Diamond knurling (Drawn at 30°)

Revise it!

Draw a threaded bar that is chamfered to help get the nut started and has a knurled handle at one end.

Remember it!

- **Thread** – a thread on the inside or outside of a part so it can fit to another.
- **Chamfer** – a sloping edge cut into the corner of two sides to improve safety.
- **Countersink** – a well for a bolt or screw head to fit flush against the surface.
- **Hole** – a connection point for bolts, screws or other components to fit into.
- **Knurl** – a patterned texture added to a material to increase grip.

Revision Guide

Working drawings: Abbreviations   see p. 92

What you need to know

- What each abbreviation refers to.

Abbreviations are used to save time and space writing out the full word. They need to be standard so that all designers can understand them.

The abbreviation is put before the number or information.

Design abbreviations

Design abbreviations according to BS 8888.

Name	Abbreviation(s)	What it means
Across Flats	AF	Distance from one flat surface to the opposite flat.
Centre Line	CL	Line that runs through the centre of the part drawn.
Diameter	DIA, D and Ø	The measurement from one side of circle to other.
Drawing	DRG	Often followed by a number to identify it.
Material	MATL	Will have a material stated after it.
Square	SQ	Number given to show size of square.

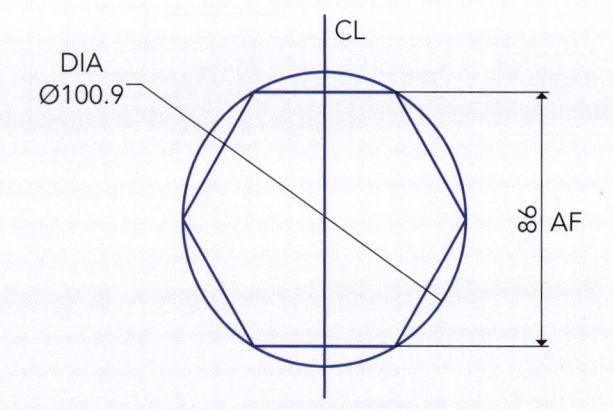

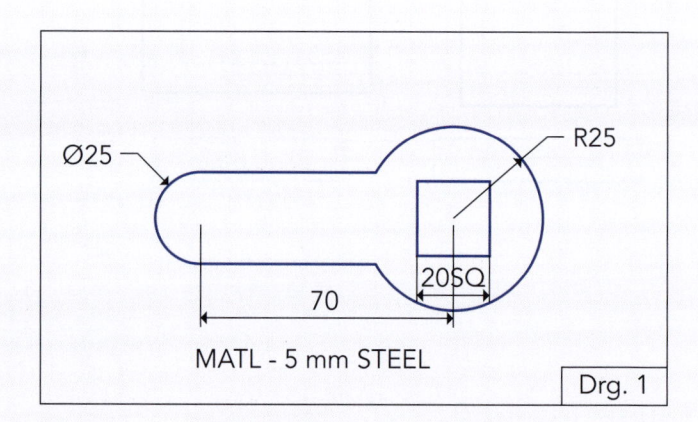

Revise it!

Create a drawing in a style of your choice then add the design abbreviations to the picture.

Remember it!

The abbreviation letters link to the definition.

For example: **AF** stands for **A**cross **F**lats

Using CAD drawing software   see p. 93

What you need to know

- Advantages and limitations of using CAD to create designs.

CAD stands for computer aided design. It is a drawing software which allows 3D models to be produced on screen with different parts and representing different materials.

Using CAD

There are many advantages and limitations of using CAD drawing software compared with manual drawing techniques.

Advantages
• Easy to edit to correct mistakes or change features. • Allows you to view your design from all angles. • Easy to quickly share around the world. • **Animation** and **simulation** can be used to model function.
Limitations
• Need skill training to use CAD. • Need to have access to a computer and CAD software. • Can hinder creativity when initially getting the idea on screen. • Work can be lost due to viruses, hacking or equipment breaking.

When CAD might be used

CAD is used for designing and modelling parts and products in many industries, including automotive, aerospace, architecture, dentistry, forensics, interior design and even fashion!

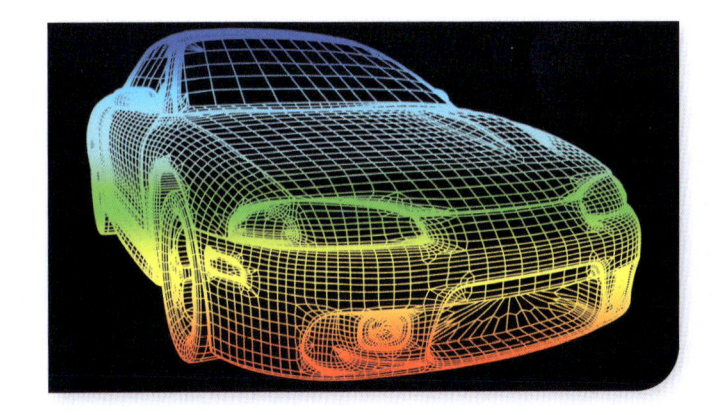

Practise it!

You are set a brief to design a new phone case.

What would be the advantages and limitations of using CAD for:

- the designer? (2 marks)
- the client? (2 marks)

Remember it!

Computer aided design (CAD) – allows 3D models to be produced on screen with different parts and modelled in different materials.

Revision Guide

57

Evaluating design ideas: Production of models see p. 94

What you need to know

- The different methods of evaluating design ideas.

When you have completed your design ideas you need to be able to evaluate them to see if they are fit for purpose.

Evaluation methods

Before a design can be finalised, it needs to be evaluated to check it is going to work.

To do this, some of the following are carried out:

- Production of models.
- **Qualitative comparison** against design brief and specification.
- Key points of the design are ranked against set matrices.
- Quality function deployment (QFD).

Production of models

Models are produced by different methods and in different materials to aid visualisation of the idea.

They help with the testing and evaluation of design ideas.

They allow the client to see a physical model and give feedback.

Result of evaluation

Some aspects of the design may change after assessing the model. For example:

- Size – it might be made bigger or smaller.
- Shape – the overall shape could be made more visually appealing.
- Material – it may be easier to produce in a different material.

Revise it!

Create a mind map to show all the benefits that you can think of to the client, designer and manufacturer of carrying out an evaluation of the designs before the design moves on to manufacture.

Remember it!

- There are different ways of evaluating.
- Evaluations are done to make sure that the design is fit for purpose before moving on to the manufacturing stage.

Evaluating design ideas: Qualitative comparisons (see p. 94)

What you need to know

- What a qualitative comparison is.
- What information is obtained by carrying out a qualitative comparison.

When you have completed your design ideas, you can carry out a qualitative comparison with the design brief and specification.

Qualitative comparison

A qualitative comparison evaluation is formulated from information collected by observations, interviews and participant opinions.

The design can be examined and compared with the design brief requirements and the points within the specification.

This allows the design to be checked against details that have been agreed with the client.

Qualitative comparisons are more about the insights of the testers than about how many testers you have.

Using a product in the environment it is designed for can provide real insight into how the product will be used, and any design alterations needed to account for scenarios in the real world. However, this method is reliant on people's opinions which are subjective and may sway the design process.

Advantages	Limitations
- Feedback can be gathered by different methods. - Does not require a large number of participants. - Allows for people's opinions, feelings and attitudes to be taken into account. - More flexible approach.	- Does not produce factual data. - More challenging to analyse results. - Opinions held by a minority of people may unduly influence the design process.

Practise it!

The cleaning products in the photograph above met all of the client's requirements during the qualitative comparison against the specification.

List *five* points that the specification would have had. **(5 marks)**

Remember it!

Qualitative comparison – information is collected through observations and interviews and by examining and comparing the design idea against the brief and specification.

Revision Guide

Evaluating design ideas: Ranking matrices see p. 94

What you need to know

- How ranking matrices are used to evaluate design ideas.

When design ideas are completed they need to be checked for conformity to set requirements before they move on to the manufacturing stage.

What is a ranking matrix?

A **ranking matrix** (plural: **ranking matrices**) can help focus an evaluation by giving set criteria to evaluate against.

The criteria are weighted to allow a score to be given to the features of the design.

Below is an example of a ranking matrix for a new kettle design.

	Size	Cost	Ease of use	Total score
Weighting of criteria (5 most important – 1 least)	5	3	4	
Idea 1 (big kettle)	4	1	2	
Rating	5 × 4 = **20**	3 × 1 = **3**	4 × 2 = **8**	**31**
Idea 2 (small kettle)	1	3	4	
Rating	5 × 1 = **5**	3 × 3 = **9**	4 × 4 = **16**	**30**

The tester will then test the product and score each feature according to the given key. That score is then multiplied by the set weighting to give an overall score.

Advantages	Disadvantages
• Criteria can be set in advance using information from the client, design brief and specification. • Allows for consistency when evaluating information from a range of testers. • Gives the designer a rating for the different design features, so can help them with development.	• Can become complex if produced for a detailed design. • Only gives numerical feedback, not ideas for development.

Revise it!

Complete the headings for a matrix for the testing of a new phone.

Give each of the points a weighting so that a tester can give the design an overall score.

Remember it!

Ranking matrices give a score for key features that are being tested.

Evaluating design ideas: Quality function deployment see p. 94

What you need to know
- What quality function deployment (QFD) is.
- How it helps the evaluation of designs.

All design ideas need to be evaluated to make sure they meet the customers' requirements.

Quality function deployment

Quality function deployment (QFD) is a method developed in Japan to transform the voice of the customer.

It defines the customers' needs and requirements so that they can be shared with different parts of the company making the product.

Customer requirements are turned into measurable design targets that can then be evaluated against during the design process.

Sometimes a matrix is used to create a grid to evaluate the ideas against the targets.

Advantages	Disadvantages
• Increases customer satisfaction by prioritising their requirements. • Improves the quality of products. • Allows for evaluation against measurable targets.	• Does not take other design factors into account, such as cost or time to produce a product. • Creating a QFD matrix can be complex and time consuming.

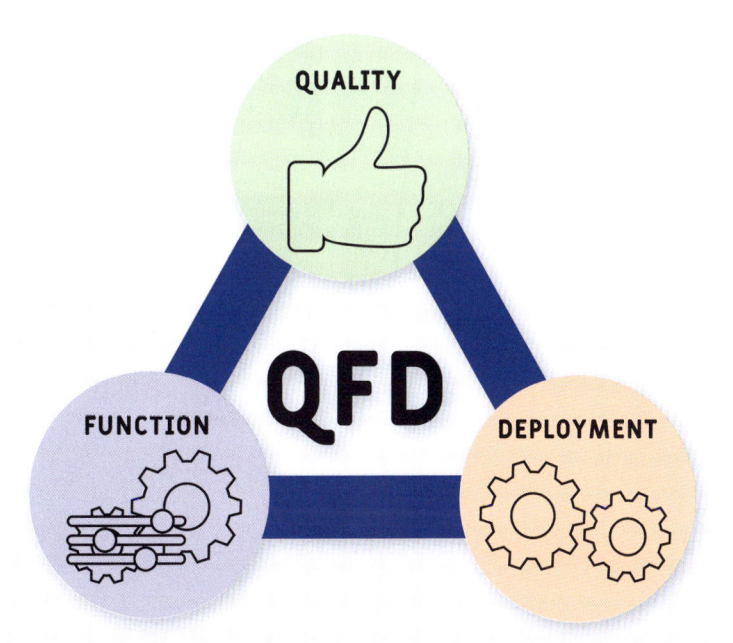

Revise it!
List *five* needs that a customer might have for a new laptop as actionable steps that can be used to evaluate designs.

Remember it!
Quality function deployment (QFD) – turning the needs of the customer into actionable steps that a design can be evaluated against.

Revision Guide

61

Modelling methods: Virtual (3D CAD) see p. 95

What you need to know

- What different types of modelling methods are used.
- What information can be obtained by using the different methods.

Virtual modelling is where a part or product is modelled in 3D using a computer aided design (CAD) package. There is no physical model.

3D CAD

Visual check on all sides of model as it can be rotated on screen.

Check if individual parts that have been designed can successfully be assembled.

Advantages	Limitations
• Design can be easily edited and adjusted on screen. • The file can be used to run a CAM process to make a physical model.	• Takes time to design the parts accurately on CAD. • Can't hold and take physical measurements.

Revise it!

Imagine you have been given a CAD file to evaluate a design.
Make a list of the advantages of having a CAD file over a hand drawn design idea.

Remember it!

- Virtual modelling – 3D CAD image.
- Allows for viewing in 360° and changes can be made instantly.

62   Revision Guide

Modelling methods: Card see p. 95

What you need to know

- Why card models are used.

Designs need to be modelled in real life to make them easier to visualise and to aid people in evaluating them fully.

Card modelling

Card modelling is a simple process that needs minimal equipment and only basic resources.

Key equipment would include a ruler, cutting mat, knife and adhesive.

Different thicknesses of card can be used to model different parts.

Finishes can be added to aid the visualisation of the idea.

Size and scale can be checked when multiple parts are modelled.

Advantages	Limitations
- Can be modelled off a hand drawn design. - Does not need expensive equipment. - Gives a visual idea of the model in 3D.	- Can be quite basic due to limitations of the material. - Tends not to allow for function to be tested.

Revise it!

Create a table with at least *four* advantages and *four* disadvantages of using card modelling over other types of **modelling**.

Remember it!

Card modelling is quick and doesn't require expensive equipment.

Revision Guide

Modelling methods: Block (see p. 95)

What you need to know

- What a block model is.
- How it is used for evaluating designs.

In order to evaluate some parts of a design idea, it is necessary to model them so that they can be visualised and also checked for function.

Block modelling

A block of material is used to create a 3D representation of the design or part of the design.

Often made of modelling foam which can be carved and shaped using basic tools.

Clear visual of the 3D shape.

Accurate size of the design.

Can check to see if ergonomic features function as intended.

Advantages	Limitations
- 3D models are produced. - Size, shape and finishes can be modelled. - Can produce curves and detailed shapes.	- Hard to produce complex models. - Doesn't normally have working features.

Revise it!

A designer makes a model of a new hand grip that will go on a new range of power tools. What will the model help the designer to find out?

Remember it!

Block modelling – model is made out of a block of material to allow shape and ergonomic features to be tested.

64 Revision Guide

Modelling methods: Breadboarding see p. 95

What you need to know

- Why breadboarding is used before creating a circuit.
- What information can be obtained by using breadbaords.

When you design circuits, you can model them on CAD but you also need to check if the chosen components will work in real life.

Breadboarding

Breadboarding is a simple method of testing circuits by pushing the component legs into the holes on the **breadboard**.

No specialised equipment is needed and the parts can be moved round and used again.

Accurate test of the function of the circuit.

Settings and values needed for some components in sensing circuits.

Advantages	Limitations
- Uses real components to check function. - Quick and easy to build and edit.	- Needs real components to test, which can cause a delay. - Increases cost if components need to be brought in specially.

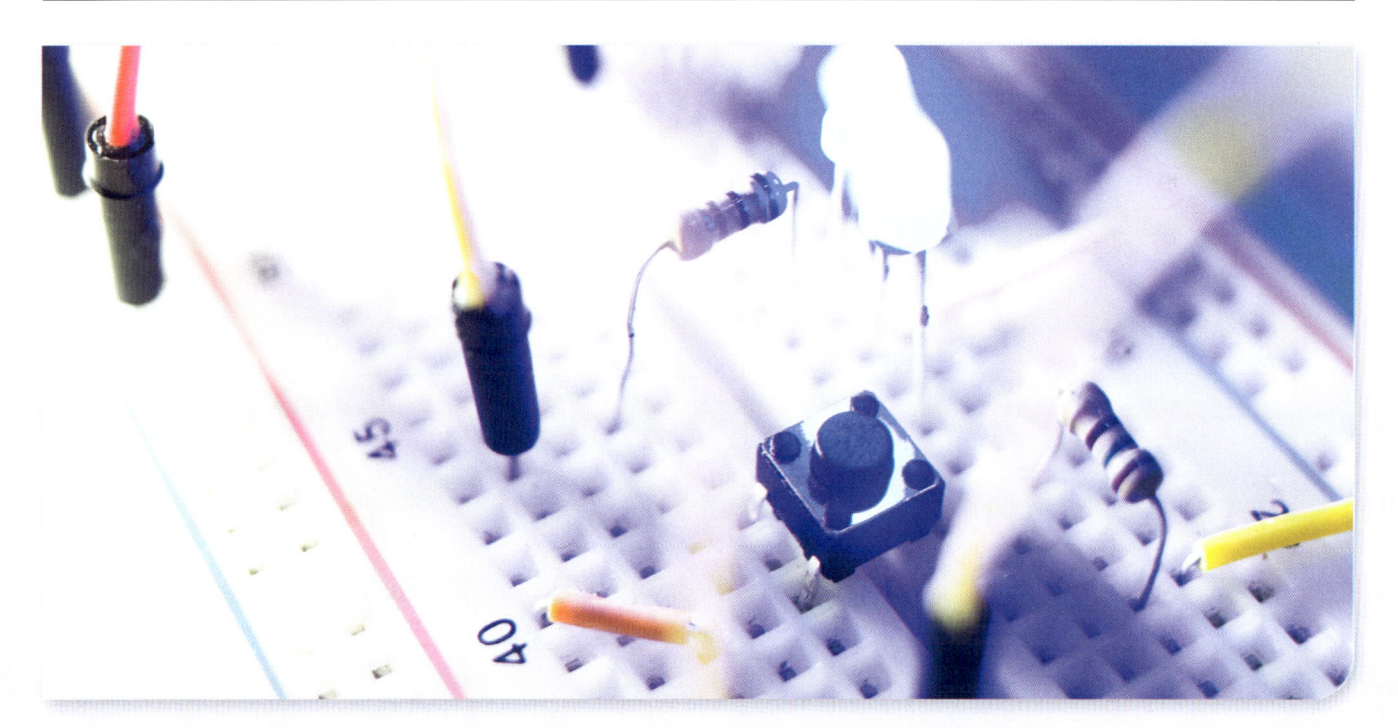

Revise it!

Create a list comparing breadboarding to CAD modelling of circuits.
What are the key differences and why are both used?

Remember it!

Breadboarding – prototyping of circuits using actual components and no heat.

Revision Guide

65

Modelling methods: 3D printing *see p. 95*

What you need to know
- What 3D printing is.
- How 3D printing is used to evaluate designs.

When designs are created, it is often hard to fully visualise and test them on screen.

3D printing methods

3D printing is an additive manufacturing technique which uses a computer-controlled machine to create a 3D model of a design. The machine produces the model using the CAD file created at the design stage.

Models can be produced in a range of materials and qualities.

Advantages	Limitations
• Get clear visual idea of design. • Can physically touch and test the model. • Fitment of parts and sizes can be checked. • Checks can be made against the specification.	• Need expensive equipment to produce the part. • Need a CAD file for the machine to work from. • Limited materials. • Prints can take a lot of time.

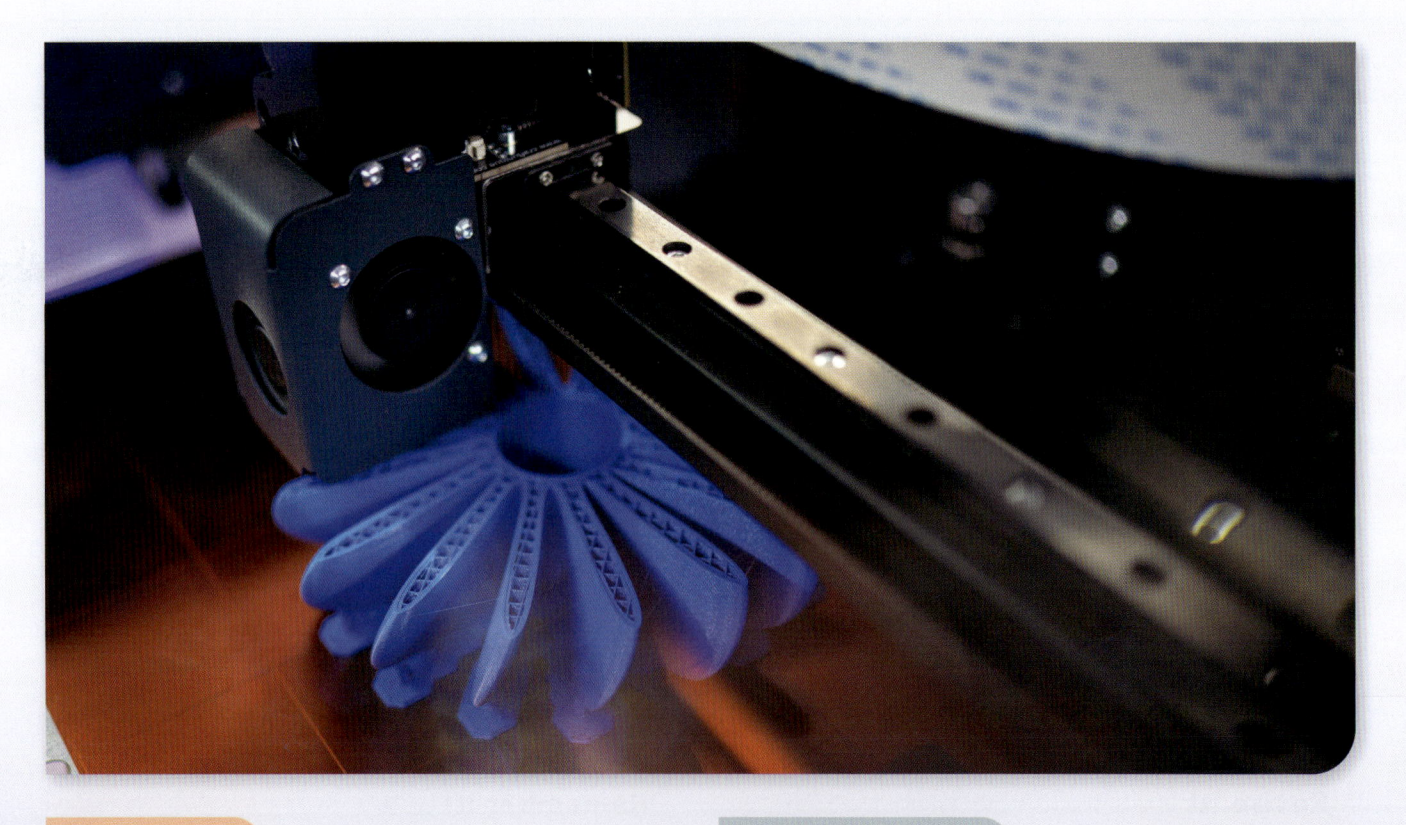

Revise it!
Create a flowchart showing the steps from designing through to creating a 3D model using a 3D printer.

Remember it!
3D printing allows for a prototype to be made to test physically.

Revision Guide

Evaluating design outcomes: Dimensions and functionality (see p. 96)

What you need to know

- Different methods used to evaluate design outcomes.
- The advantages and limitations of each method.

When you have made a model of a design idea, you need to test and accurately evaluate it against the requirements to identify any areas that need modification.

Methods of evaluating a design outcome

There are many methods of evaluating a design outcome and obtaining factual data and results that can be acted upon to modify and develop the design.

- Checking the dimensions and function of the product.
- **Quantitative comparison** against the design brief and specification.
- Information found through user testing.

Measuring dimensions and functionality

- Models are measured against drawings and also specification requirements.
- Moving or functioning parts of model are tested for fit and function.
- Measuring must be accurate so equipment such as Vernier callipers, steel rulers and micrometers can be used.

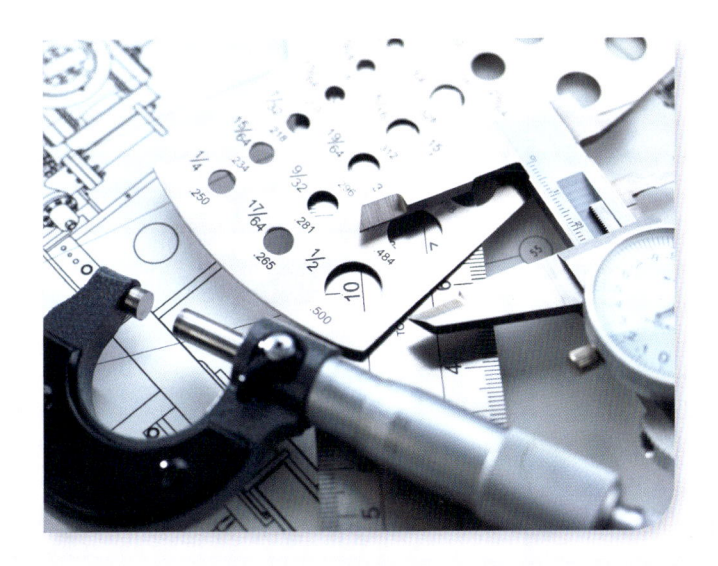

Advantages	Limitations
- Get factual data to evaluate. - Can spot issues before final products are made. - Can test if the design idea functions as intended.	- It may not be possible to measure some internal details on a 3D model. - Depending on the modelling method, not all functions may be tested.

Practise it!

You have created a new design for a light to fit on a bike.

- What forms of modelling would be best for the testing? **(2 marks)**
- What features would need measuring and testing? **(2 marks)**

Remember it!

- Measuring – must be accurate to make it useful for the evaluation.
- Functionality must be tested to see if it meets the specification requirements.

Revision Guide 67

Evaluating design outcomes: Quantitative comparison see p. 96

What you need to know

- What a quantitative comparison is compared against.
- The advantages and limitations of quantitative comparisons.

When evaluating ideas, it is important to collect factual data that can be analysed.

Quantitative comparison

A quantitative comparison can be carried out against the design brief and the specification.

It compares the design idea and model against factual data within the specification.

The results are easy to analyse and summarise as they are all based on numbers.

The data produced can be represented clearly in charts, graphs and tables for feedback to the customer.

Advantages	Limitations
- Produces data by comparing results with the required facts in the specification. - Allows for factual data to be used and analysed. - Data can be gathered by different methods.	- Requires specific data to be included in the specification, which can then be evaluated against. - Feedback is limited to factual data – there can be no analysis of people's opinions, feelings or attitudes.

Practise it!

You are evaluating a design for a new bike.

List *five* things that could have been included in the specification that will give quantitative results for the evaluation. **(5 marks)**

Remember it!

Quantitative comparison – design is compared against specific points to give factual data.

Evaluating design outcomes: User testing (see p. 96)

What you need to know

- Why user testing is important.
- What data can be found from user testing.

User testing is an important part of design development. If the design idea and model are tested and found to be unsuitable for the users they are aimed at, the final product will not be a success.

Hands-on testing

By making a functioning model to demonstrate the design idea, you are then able to carry out hands-on user testing. This can be a full working prototype or just an element, like a case shape or handle grip.

Advantages	Limitations
- Different types of data can be collected. - Can check that the size and shape are correct. - If using set questions, can collect data to analyse.	- Will need a good model to allow for user testing. - Need to collect a range of data so need to be able to allow more than one user to test it.

Revise it!

Look around the room. Select a product you can see.

- List *five* things that you as a user think are good points.
- List *five* things that you as a user think could do with improvement.

Then think about how, as a designer, you could act on this feedback.

Remember it!

- User testing is important to check if the idea really meets the design brief.
- User testing relies on some form of model that can be examined and tested.

Revision Guide

Evaluating design outcomes: Modifications and improvements   see p. 96

What you need to know

- Why it is important to look at possible modifications and improvements to design ideas.

No design is ever perfect first time. Using testing and evaluation results allow the designer to identify changes that may be needed.

Potential improvements

After testing and evaluating a design idea, you should have data and feedback that will help you identify potential modifications to the design that will improve its function.

These developments are important to make sure the product is fit for purpose and safe for the user to use as intended.

Advantages	Limitations
- Modifications and improvements can be made before the product goes into production; this saves money. - Modifications can be made quickly using CAD and then if 3D printed can be reprinted for retesting.	- If larger modifications need to be made after testing then the design and testing process may need to be repeated. - Depending on how the model was made, it could be time consuming to remodel with modifications.

Revise it!

Look at this picture.

What modifications might have been passed to the designer after testing?

Think about how ergonomic the handles are because they have been user tested.

Remember it!

- No design is perfect; designers must be open to act on feedback so that the design can be modified and improved.
- They can check against the design brief, specification and user testing feedback.

Revision Guide

Design strategies: Linear design (see p. 19)

1 Describe what is meant by the linear design process. **(2 marks)**

....

....

....

....

2 Identify *three* stages of the linear design process that are completed before the development of a final design. One has been done for you. **(3 marks)**

- *Design brief* ....

- ....

- ....

3 State *two* advantages and *one* disadvantage of linear design. **(3 marks)**

Advantage: ....

....

....

Advantage: ....

....

....

Disadvantage: ....

....

....

Design strategies: Iterative design see p. 20

1 Using a labelled diagram, describe the stages of the iterative design process. **(4 marks)**

2 Explain *two* advantages of the iterative design process. **(4 marks)**

- ....
  ....
  ....
- ....
  ....
  ....

3 Describe *one* example of the use of iterative design. **(3 marks)**

....
....
....

Design strategies: Inclusive design (see p. 21)

1. Complete this table by giving *four* examples of inclusive design and explaining how each is inclusive. One has been done for you. **(8 marks)**

Example of inclusive design	How it is inclusive
Toothbrush with curvy handle	*Easy for children to hold*

2. State *two* advantages and *two* disadvantages of inclusive design. **(4 marks)**

Advantage: ....

....

Advantage: ....

....

Disadvantage: ....

....

Disadvantage: ....

....

Design strategies: User-centred design (see p. 22)

1 State what is placed at the heart of user-centred design. **(1 mark)**

....

2 State how often user feedback is collected during a user-centred design process. **(1 mark)**

....

3 State the main disadvantage to user-centred design when trying to create a commercial product. **(1 mark)**

....

Design strategies: Sustainable design (see p. 23)

1 State the type of resources that will run out if we don't embrace sustainable design. **(1 mark)**

....

2 State *two* ways to make sure a design is sustainable. **(2 marks)**

- ....

    ....

- ....

    ....

Design strategies: Ergonomic design *see p. 24*

1 Complete the following sentence: (2 marks)

Ergonomic design is about ensuring that users can interact with

.... and .... products.

2 Circle ◯ the correct ending to this sentence:

Ergonomic design involves consideration of how people … (1 mark)

   A … recycle products.

   B … interact with products.

   C … shop for products.

Iterative design: Analysis of the design brief *see p. 25*

1 Explain *one* reason why it is important to analyse a design brief. (2 marks)

....

....

....

....

Iterative design: Methods of researching the product requirements (see p. 26)

1 Identify the *two* types of research. **(2 marks)**

- ....
- ....

2 State *three* methods of collecting primary research. **(3 marks)**

- ....
- ....
- ....

3 State *three* sources where secondary research can be found. **(3 marks)**

- ....
- ....
- ....

4 Identify the potential benefits to a designer of analysing and disassembling an existing product. **(2 marks)**

....

....

....

....

5 Describe what anthropometric data is and how it helps designers. **(2 marks)**

....

....

....

....

Iterative design: Producing an engineering design specification see p. 27

1. The design specification contains specific facts and features that the design must meet.

   Some topics covered in the specification are size and safety.

   Identify *three* others that might be included. One has been done for you. **(3 marks)**

   - *aesthetics*
   - ....
   - ....

2. The design specification required this toothbrush to be designed with user-centred design. Identify which areas of the design may meet these criteria. **(2 marks)**

   - ....
   - ....

Iterative design: Generating design ideas by sketching and modelling see p. 28

1. Complete these sentences by choosing words from the list. **(2 marks)**

CAD	modify	sketching	model	disassembling

   - A designer may be asked to design a new product or .... an existing design.
   - The quickest way for a designer to record ideas is by ....

Iterative design: Modelling ideas see pp. 29–32

1 By modelling a design idea, the designer can test its scale.

State *two* other things that can be tested once a model has been made. **(2 marks)**

- ....

- ....

2 State the *two* different types of modelling. **(2 marks)**

- V ....

- P ....

3 Outline the benefits to the designer of using CAD to model a design. **(4 marks)**

....

....

....

....

....

....

4 A physical model of a design idea can help the designer to visualise the idea fully.

It can also help with testing.

Identify *two* materials that are often used to produce physical models. **(2 marks)**

- ....

- ....

5 Circle ◯ the correct ending to this sentence:

Physical models are made … **(1 mark)**

A … full size.

B … to scale.

C … both full size and to scale.

6 A design is tested and compared with the requirements of the design brief and specification. It is found to not meet the requirements fully.

What happens next? Tick (✓) the correct response (1 mark)

   A The design is then manufactured. ☐

   B The design is then modified. ☐

7 Explain, with examples, *two* reasons why it is important that modifications are picked up during the design and modification stage. (4 marks)

....

....

....

....

....

....

Design criteria: Needs and wants see p. 33

1 What is a 'specification'? (2 marks)

....

....

2 Explain the term 'needs' in relation to design specifications. (2 marks)

....

....

....

....

3 Explain the term 'wants' in relation to design specifications. (2 marks)

....

....

....

Design criteria: Quantitative and qualitative see p. 34

1 Fill in this table for a bicycle by identifying *three* needs and *three* wants that the user might have. Two have been done for you. **(6 marks)**

User's needs	User's wants
To have adjustable seat height with movement of 100 mm.	*Padding in the saddle to keep rider comfortable.*

2 For the bike, identify *two* points – either new ones or the ones you have given above – that are quantitative, and *two* points that are qualitative. **(4 marks)**

Quantitative:

- ....
- ....

Qualitative:

- ....
- ....

80 Workbook

Design criteria: ACCESS FM (see p. 35)

1 Complete this table to explain why points from ACCESS FM are used in specification criteria. **(4 marks)**

Why is it necessary to include information about these points in a specification? Give examples in your explanations.

Customer	
Material	

Manufacturing considerations: Scale (see p. 36)

1 Circle ◯ the item that is classed as one-off. **(1 mark)**

   A Football stadium   B Mobile phone   C Car

2 Circle ◯ the item that is produced through batch production. **(1 mark)**

   A Bridge   B Screws   C Circuit board

3 Circle ◯ the mass-produced item. **(1 mark)**

   A Handmade sideboard   B Bridge   C Bolts

4 Outline why the scale in which a product is going to be made will affect the way it is designed. **(2 marks)**

   ....
   ....
   ....
   ....

Workbook

Manufacturing considerations: Availability and form (see p. 37)

1. Describe how material availability will affect the possible design solutions. **(3 marks)**

....

....

....

....

2. Materials are manufactured in standard forms.

   Outline why this needs to be considered by designers when designing new products. **(2 marks)**

....

....

....

....

Manufacturing considerations: Processes (see p. 38)

1. Complete this table. Four have been done for you. **(8 marks)**

Process	Description
Wasting	
	Soldering parts together.
	Adding paint to a product.
Assembly	

82 Workbook

Manufacturing considerations: Production costs see p. 39

1 State the *two* key areas of production costs that need to be considered
   when designing. **(2 marks)**

   • ....
   ....

   • ....
   ....

2 Outline why it is important to take costs into account when designing
   a new product. **(3 marks)**

   ....
   ....
   ....
   ....
   ....

Influences on product design: Pull and push see p. 40

1 Complete these *two* terms that are an influence on the development of
   new designs. **(2 marks)**

   (a) .... pull

   (b) Technology ....

2 Complete this paragraph:

   A new processing chip has been designed to make a faster computer.
   This means that a new product can be designed.

   This is called .... **(1 mark)**

Workbook

3 Complete this paragraph:

Consumer demand has caused a company to look at designing a new product.

This is called .... **(1 mark)**

Influences on product design: Standards see p. 41

1 Fill in the gap:

BS 8888 is a .... Standard. **(1 mark)**

2 Fill in the gaps:

ISO standards are created by the ....

for .... **(2 marks)**

3 The CE mark on products is being replaced by the UKCA mark.

(a) State what UKCA stands for. **(1 mark)**

....

....

(b) Outline why the UKCA mark is an important mark for customers to see on a product. **(1 mark)**

....

....

Influences on product design: Legislation (see p. 42)

1. Describe what 'legislation' is. (1 mark)

2. Outline what can happen to a company if it is found to have broken legislation. (1 mark)

3. State what HASAWA stands for. (1 mark)

4. Describe why legislation that relates to health and safety and risk assessments might influence design. The answer has been started for you. (3 marks)

   Companies must follow risk assessments to protect the workforce. This means that some design concepts can't be made if the processes are not suitable and safe.

Workbook

Influences on product design: Planned obsolescence (see p. 43)

1. State *two* ways in which products can become obsolete. **(2 marks)**

   - ....
   ....

   - ....
   ....

2. A product is said to have been designed with 'planned obsolescence' in mind.

   State what this means for the product. **(1 mark)**

   ....
   ....

3. State *one* advantage to the manufacturer when a product is designed with planned obsolescence. **(1 mark)**

   ....
   ....

4. Explain why planned obsolescence can be bad for the environment. **(2 marks)**

   ....
   ....
   ....

Influences on product design: Sustainable design and the circular economy see p. 44

1 Complete this table to describe each of the 6Rs of sustainable design. One has been done for you. (6 marks)

Rethink	
Reuse	
Recycle	
Repair	*Save the user money by mending an item.*
Reduce	
Refuse	

2 Identify the *three* main steps to a circular economy. (3 marks)

- ....
- ....
- ....

Workbook 87

Types of drawing see pp. 45–49

1 State *one* advantage of using freehand sketching to produce initial ideas. **(1 mark)**

   ....

   ....

2 Complete the isometric sketch of a cube. **(3 marks)**

3 State an advantage of an isometric drawing over an oblique drawing. **(1 mark)**

   ....

   ....

4 Circle ◯ the correct ending to this sentence:

   A drawing showing all of the parts of a product and how they connect
   to each other is called … **(1 mark)**

   A … an isometric drawing.

   B … a block diagram.

   C … an exploded view.

5 Circle ◯ the correct ending to this sentence:

   Assembly drawings show the client … **(1 mark)**

   A … what colour the product will be.

   B … what parts of the product will look like when they are assembled.

   C … the overall size of the finished item.

88 Workbook

6 A block diagram is an easy way to draw a basic system.

Complete the block diagram and add a feedback line. **(5 marks)**

7 A basic flowchart has *three* main box shapes. Draw them and state what each one means. **(3 marks)**

8 Circle ◯ the correct ending to this sentence:

A circuit diagram shows how components are joined together in circuits by using … **(1 mark)**

 A … standard symbols.

 B … pictures of the components.

9 Circle ◯ the type of diagram that would be used to show how a socket in a house is wired. **(1 mark)**

 A Circuit diagram

 B Orthographic drawing

 C Wiring diagram

Workbook

Working drawings: Third angle orthographic projection and standard conventions see pp. 50–51

1 List *two* important pieces of information that a title block on a working drawing tells the manufacturer. **(2 marks)**

   - ....
   - ....

2 A drawing has a scale stated on it. What does that tell you?
   Circle ◯ the correct answer. **(1 mark)**

   A The drawing is the exact size of the part.

   B The drawing has been accurately enlarged or reduced compared with the part to make the picture fit the paper.

3 A part that needs to be made 35 mm long has a stated tolerance of ± 0.5 mm.

   Circle ◯ *two* acceptable measurements for the part. **(2 marks)**

   A 34.8 mm

   B 35.7 mm

   C 34.4 mm

   D 35.2 mm

4 Draw the symbol for a third angle orthographic drawing. **(2 marks)**

90 Workbook

Working drawings: Dimensions see p. 52

1 This shape has a width of 160 mm and a height of 70 mm and the circle has a radius of 20 mm.

   Using standard conventions for dimensions, label the drawing. (3 marks)

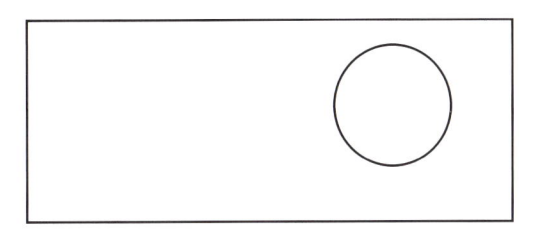

Working drawings: Line types see p. 53

1 Complete the table by drawing the lines that you would expect to see on a diagram to represent outline, centre line and hidden detail. (3 marks)

Outline	
Centre line	
Hidden detail	

Working drawings: Mechanical features see p. 54

1 Complete the diagram to show:

   (a) a 45° chamfer on both ends (1 mark)

   (b) diamond knurling into the left-hand end (1 mark)

   (c) external threading on the bar. (1 mark)

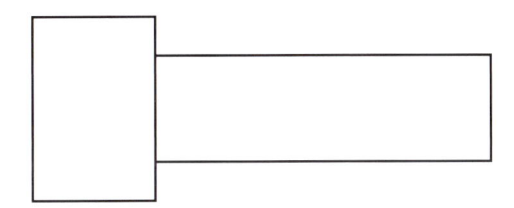

Workbook 91

2 Draw an example of a Ø10 mm countersink into a Ø5 mm hole in a piece of 10 mm thick aluminium block.

Show all the detail you would expect to see if the drawing was given to you. **(4 marks)**

Working drawings: Abbreviations (see p. 56)

1 Complete this table of abbreviations used on engineering drawings. **(5 marks)**

Abbreviation	Definition
DIA	
MATL	
DRG	Drawing
	Square
AF	
	Centre Line

92 Workbook

Using CAD drawing software (see p. 57)

1 Describe, with examples, why CAD software can benefit a designer.
   One example has been given for you. **(4 marks)**

   Using CAD software, a designer can share their design ideas with other people quickly and easily. This allows others to collaborate on the design.

   ....

   ....

   ....

   ....

   ....

   ....

   ....

   ....

2 State *two* advantages of using CAD software compared with drawing by hand. **(2 marks)**

   • ....

   ....

   • ....

   ....

3 State *two* limitations of using CAD software compared with drawing by hand. **(2 marks)**

   • ....

   ....

   • ....

   ....

Workbook 93

Evaluating design ideas see pp. 58–61

1. State *two* benefits to the designer of producing models of their ideas. **(2 marks)**

   • ....

   ....

   • ....

   ....

2. What *two* documents can quantitative comparisons be carried out against? **(2 marks)**

   • ....

   • ....

3. Explain why ranking matrices are useful to designers during testing and evaluation of design ideas. **(3 marks)**

   ....

   ....

   ....

   ....

   ....

   ....

4. Describe how QFD can help when evaluating design ideas. **(2 marks)**

   ....

   ....

   ....

Modelling methods see pp. 62–66

1. Circle ◯ *two* modelling methods that a chair designer could use to model an ergonomic stool top. **(2 marks)**

   A Breadboard

   B CAD

   C Block

   D Card

2. Describe *two* advantages and *two* disadvantages of using CAD to virtually model a part. **(4 marks)**

   Advantage: ....

   ....

   Advantage: ....

   ....

   Disadvantage: ....

   ....

   Disadvantage: ....

   ....

3. Identify the type of design that can be modelled using breadboarding. **(1 mark)**

   ....

4. State *two* pieces of information that a designer can gain from a 3D printed model of a design idea. **(2 marks)**

   - ....

   - ....

5. Card modelling is an inexpensive way to make a model.

   Explain *one* advantage and *one* disadvantage of using card to model your design ideas. **(4 marks)**

   Advantage: ....

   ....

   Disadvantage: ....

   ....

Evaluating design outcomes see pp. 67–70

1. List *two* pieces of equipment that can be used to measure the dimensions of a model against the working drawing. One has been done for you. **(2 marks)**

   - *Vernier callipers*
   - ....

2. State the type of information that quantitative comparisons give a designer. **(1 mark)**

   ....

   ....

3. Explain the benefit to the designer of doing a quantitative comparison of the idea against the design brief and the specification. **(3 marks)**

   ....

   ....

   ....

   ....

4. Designers create physical models and then carry out user testing to find out key information.

   Explain *two* benefits and *two* limitations of this type of testing. **(4 marks)**

   Benefit: ....

   ....

   Benefit: ....

   ....

   Limitation: ....

   ....

   Limitation: ....

   ....

5 Designers need to modify and improve ideas by using testing and evaluations to gather feedback.

Explain why it is so important to identify improvements and modifications when designing new products. **(4 marks)**

Glossary

Key terms

2D: Two dimensional (flat) components with features defined using X and Y coordinates.

3D: Three dimensional components with features defined using X, Y and Z coordinates.

Abbreviation: A shortened form of a word or phrase. In engineering design, it is often a letter or symbol used to represent a design feature.

ACCESS FM: Mnemonic for remembering and describing the key points covered by a design specification. Stands for:

- Aesthetics
- Cost
- Customer
- Environment
- Size
- Safety
- Function
- Materials

Aesthetics: The way a product reacts with the senses, defining pleasing qualities.

Animation: Method to create the illusion of movement.

Anthropometrics: The study of measurements of the human body.

Anthropometrist: A scientist who deals with anthropometry: the measurement of the size, weight and proportions of the human body.

Assembly: A process of fitting components together to make a whole product.

Assembly drawing: Drawing showing how separate components fit together.

Batch production: Manufacturing products in specific amounts (a batch).

Block diagram: Diagram of products or systems where separate parts are represented by blocks connected by lines showing their relationship to one another.

Block modelling: Using blocks of material to create a 3D representation of a design or part of a design.

Breadboard: Used to build and test circuits quickly before finalising any circuit design.

Breadboarding: A way of testing electronic circuits on a solderless construction base called a breadboard.

British Standards: Standards that products must conform to, produced by the BSI (British Standards Institution).

Cabinet oblique: A method of representing a 3D object on paper by extending the depth of the drawing using lines at 45 degrees. The receding axis (the depth) is drawn at half size to appear visually similar to the object.

Capital costs: Starting costs of setting up a facility to manufacture a product.

Card modelling: Using card to create real-life models; needs minimal equipment and only basic resources.

Cavalier oblique: A method of representing a 3D object on paper by extending the depth of the drawing using lines at 45 degrees. The receding axis (the depth) is drawn at full size.

Circuit diagram: Graphical representation of an electric circuit, showing how separate electrical components are connected to one another.

Circular economy: A system that reduces the impact of products on the environment by reducing waste and pollution and maximising the reuse of materials.

Computer aided design (CAD): Software that allows 3D models to be produced on screen with different parts and modelled in different materials.

Computer aided manufacture (CAM): Use of software to control machine tools in manufacturing.

Design brief: A short summary of the design context and the main user requirements.

Design specification: A detailed list that gives clear and specific requirements for the product being designed so it can match the design brief. See also: ACCESS FM.

Design strategy: A method for designing a product.

Diameter: Distance across a circle.

Dimensions: Numerical values used in engineering drawings to specify the sizes or positions of key features (measurements are usually in millimetres).

Disassembly: Taking something apart, for example, a piece of equipment or a product; often to repair, replace or recycle components.

Ergonomics: Arranging or designing a product in a way that enables people to interact with it more efficiently or safely, often using anthropometric data as a reference.

Ergonomic design: The design of anything that involves people.

Evaluation: Checking a design or product to ensure it will work as intended and matches the design brief and specification.

Exploded view: Drawing where the components of a product are drawn slightly separated from each other and suspended in space to show their relationship or the order of assembly.

Finishing: A process that changes the surface of a material in a useful way, either protective or decorative.

Flowchart: Block diagram that shows how various processes are linked together to achieve a specific outcome.

Forming: A process that changes the shape of a material without a change of state.

Freehand sketching: Drawing without the use of measuring instruments.

Functional anthropometry: The recording of measurements taken from body positions when moving or undertaking an activity. For example, the reach or angle of rotation when moving arms to complete a task or the dimensions of a person in a crawling stance.

Inclusive design: Designing products to be usable by as many different people as possible without special modifications.

International Standards: Standards created by the ISO (International Organization for Standardization).

Isometric drawing: 3D pictorial drawing that focuses on the edge of an object and uses an angle of 30° to the horizontal.

Iterative design: The development of a product through modelling and repeated testing.

Joining: A process that is used to attach separate pieces of material together.

Labour costs: Costs of paying people to make a product.

Legislation: Laws proposed by the government and made official by Acts of Parliament.

Linear design: The development of a product through a series of sequential stages.

Linear measurements: Show the measurements of a part or product, usually in mm. Marked with lines and arrows.

Longevity: The useful life of a product, from manufacture until its eventual disposal.

Machined finish: The surface roughness left on a material after shaping it with a cutting tool. Measured in μm.

Manufacturing processes: Processes that are used to make products.

Market pull: When a need for a product arises from consumer demand which 'pulls' the development of a new product.

Mass production: Rapid production of standardised products and components, often on a production line.

Mechanical features: Common features of a product's or component's shape or form, such as holes, threads, chamfers, countersinks and knurls; displayed on drawings using standard markings so they are easy to identify.

Model: A three-dimensional object that demonstrates the look and feel of a design.

Modelling: Creating a three-dimensional object that demonstrates the look and feel of a design and allows the designer to check the proportions, scale and function of the design.

Needs: Characteristics that a product must have.

Objective: Unbiased. For example, objective measurements are results that are taken impartially.

Oblique drawing: 3D pictorial drawing that focuses on the face of an object and uses an angle of 45° to the horizontal.

One-off production: Manufacturing products one at a time.

Orthographic drawing (projection): Working drawing that shows an object from every angle to help manufacturers plan production. Uses several 2D projections (or views) to represent a 3D object.

Physical modelling: Creating a real model using a range of materials including card, clay, wood and additive manufacturing.

Planned obsolescence: A policy of producing consumer goods that rapidly become obsolete, due to changes in design or stopping supply of spare parts.

Primary research: Research that deals directly with potential or existing customers. It can include surveys, focus groups and interviews.

Production costs: Overall costs of making a product.

Product requirements: Features a product should have or include, identified from research and described in the design specification.

Prosecuted: Officially accused in a court of breaking the law.

Prototype: A model of a product used to test the design idea to see if it functions as intended.

Qualitative: Data based on descriptions, observations or opinions.

Qualitative comparison: Gathering data from observations and interviews (with the client, customers or other engineers) and comparing with the design brief and specification.

Quality function deployment (QFD): A design tool that helps transform the customers' needs and wants into a product design and a method for evaluating design ideas.

Quantitative: Data based on numerical facts.

Quantitative comparison: Comparing numerical data from a model against factual data within the design brief and specification.

Radius: The distance from the centre of a circle to its edge.

Ranking matrix: A tool used when comparing products or when evaluating a product or design idea; provides set criteria for evaluation (plural: Ranking matrices).

Reusability: Using an object again, for its original intended purpose or for an alternative use.

Risk assessment: Identifies risks and describes ways and procedures to stop accidents happening.

Scale: Amount by which a drawing is enlarged or reduced from the actual size of an object, shown as a ratio.

Scale of manufacture: The quantity of product/parts to be made, which determines the manufacturing process.

Secondary research: Research that is based on data or insights that have already been gathered; often publicly available.

Shaping: A process that involves a change of state of the material.

Simulation: Imitation of a real product by looks and function.

Sketch: Freehand drawing used as part of the design ideas for a product.

Standard conventions: Agreed rules that set the drawing standards used in engineering, e.g., BS EN 8888.

Structural anthropometry: The recording of physical measurements of the body. For example, the height of a body when standing or sitting, or the weight of a body.

Subjective: Based upon personal opinion or preference.

Surface finish (machining): Engineered surface finish is the smoothness or roughness of the face of a material.

Sustainable design: The development of a product that uses environmentally friendly methods to not harm people or the planet.

Technology push: When new technology is created, it can lead to the development of new products that are 'pushed' onto the market.

Third angle orthographic projection: A drawing showing three different views of a part in 2D (front, plan and side) on the same diagram.

Title block: Area on a drawing which contains important information about the drawing or part.

Tolerance: The variation allowed between a specified dimension in an engineering design and the measured dimension on the finished component.

User-centred design (UCD): The development of a product to meet the requirements of a specific user or small group of users.

Virtual modelling: A computer generated representation of a design created using CAD software.

Wants: Characteristics that are desirable in a product but not essential.

Wasting: A process that removes material.

Wiring diagram: Simplified pictorial representation of a circuit to show how the components should be connected together.

Command words

Analyse: Separate or break down information into parts and identify their characteristics or elements. Explain the pros and cons of a topic or argument and make reasoned comments. Explain the impacts of actions using a logical chain of reasoning.

Annotate: Add information, for example, to a table, diagram or graph until it is final. Add all the needed or appropriate parts.

Calculate: Get a numerical answer showing how it has been worked out.

Choose: Select an answer from options given.

Circle: Select an answer from options given.

Compare and contrast: Give an account of the similarities and differences between two or more items or situations.

Complete: Add all the needed or appropriate parts. Add information, for example, to a table, diagram or graph until it is final.

Create: Produce a visual solution to a problem (for example: a mind map, flowchart or visualisation).

Describe: Give an account including all the relevant characteristics, qualities or events. Give a detailed account of.

Discuss: Present, analyse and evaluate relevant points (for example, for/against an argument).

Draw: Produce a picture or diagram.

Evaluate: Make a reasoned qualitative judgement considering different factors and using available knowledge/experience.

Explain: Give reasons for and/or causes of. Use words or phrases such as 'because', 'therefore' or 'this means that' in answers.

Fill in: Add all the needed or appropriate parts. Add information, for example, to a table, diagram or graph until it is final.

Identify: Select an answer from options given. Recognise, name or provide factors or features.

Justify: Give good reasons for offering an opinion or reaching a conclusion.

Label: Add information, for example, to a table, diagram or graph until it is final. Add all the necessary or appropriate parts.

Outline: Give a short account, summary or description.

State: Give factors or features. Give short, factual answers.

Answers

The answer pages contain examples of answers that could be given to the questions from the Revision Guide and Workbook. There may be other acceptable answers.

Practise it! activities (19–70)

Page 24

- Clear sketch (1); Labelling on sketch (1); Some form of extra grip for ease of use (1). **(3)**
- Seat shape alterations to improve comfort (1); Curved back support to improve comfort (1). **(2)**

Page 27

Any *four* from:
- Must have an opening method that is accessible to all users. (1)
- Must be made of a food safe material. (1)
- Must be recyclable when finished with. (1)
- Be easy to store and transport in large quantities. (1)
- Must be cost effective to manufacture. (1)
- Must be a standard size to reduce manufacturing costs. (1)
- Any other suitable answers. **(4)**

Page 31

Eco friendly packaging: Physical modelling in card (or similar) (1); Can be built and tested in similar way to final product (1) OR Can test for function (1). **(2)**

Handle grip: Physical modelling in clay or additive manufacture/3D printed (1); Allows for hands-on testing to test grip and comfort (1). **(2)**

Page 32

- Virtual / CAD **(1)**
- Physical modelling **(1)**

Page 34

- Quantitative: Any *three* from: Sizes (1); Quantities (1); Costs (1); Weights (1); Time (1).
- Qualitative: Any *three* from: Users' wants (1); functions (1); colours (1); shapes (1); textures (1). **(6)**

Page 38

For each product selected, any *three* of the following that are relevant: **(6)**
- Shaping – e.g. bodyboard shape created. (1)
- Forming – e.g. vacuum forming hard plastic suitcases. (1)
- Joining – most products will have parts joined together. (1)
- Finishing – adding paint to products such as chair and car. (1)
- Assembly – for any product that has more than one part. (1)

Page 40

Technology pull (1). Most customers don't actually need the newer technology (1). Technology development draws in users to upgrade (1). **(3)**

Page 41

- Any *two* from: Higher quality (1); Safer (1); More sustainable (1); Products meet set guidelines (1). **(2)**
- Good quality no matter where product is made (1); Products meet same safety standards (1). **(2)**
- Letters drawn in correct layout. **(1)**

Page 42

Any *three* from:
- Plastic bottle will not break if dropped, which could damage to surfaces (1) or cause liquid to spill onto people (1).

Answers: Practise it! activities 103

- Safety lid stops young people being able to get lid off (1) and prevents possible poisoning (1).
- Anti-spill spout to aid user by controlling pouring to avoid content splashing on hands or clothes (1).
- Gloves ensure liquid does not injure the user's skin (1). **(3)**

Page 43

- Advantage to designer – new product will need designing (1); Advantage to manufacturer – they will need to make newer versions so keeps the factory busy (1); Advantage to consumer – they have reason to upgrade (1). **(3)**
- Disadvantages: Forces people to have to spend money and upgrade (1); Products are difficult and expensive to repair, forcing consumers to upgrade instead upgrade (1); Bad for the environment (1). **(3)**

Page 46

- Drawn with the front straight on (1); lines going off at 45° (1). **(2)**
- You cannot see all of the sides (1) OR you can't see the 3D shape of the front (1). **(1)**
- Orthographic drawing would allow you to see all sides (1), and any hidden detail (1). **(2)**

Page 52

- From centre of circle to the edge. **(1)**
- From one side of circle to other, through centre (1); Ø (1). **(2)**
- No (1); the radius is half the diameter (1) so either can be calculated from the other. **(2)**

Page 57

Advantages to designer (any *one* of the following): Easy to edit design (1); Can see all sides (1); Easy to share and collaborate with other people (1).

Limitations to designer (any *one* of the following): Need training (1); Can limit creativity when trying to model ideas the design on screen (1). **(2)**

Advantages to client (any *one* of the following): Can see product in 3D (1); Don't have to be local as design can be sent to them electronically (1); Changes can be seen instantly (1).

Limitations to client (any *one* of the following): Can't touch the design (1); Doesn't always have realistic finishes (1). **(2)**

Page 59

Example answer: **(5)**
- Be a bright range of colours to be attractive to a younger market (1).
- Be made of materials that can be cleaned / sanitised easily (1).
- Have ergonomic shapes to make them comfortable for the user (1).
- Be suitable for mass production (injection moulded) (1).
- Have a design that makes it obvious how to use it correctly (1).

Page 67

- Any *two* of: 3D printed (1); block/foam (1), breadboarding (for circuit) (1). **(2)**
- Need to measure and test any *two* of: Light quality (1); Attachment method (1); Overall size (1); What range of bike sizes will it fit (1). **(2)**

Page 68

Any *five* of the following: Frame size – maximum and minimum (1); Gear numbers / ratios (1); Overall weight (1); Wheel sizes (1); Overall width of the handlebars (1); Height adjustment available on bike (1). **(5)**

Workbook 71–97

Page 71 Design strategies: Linear design

1. Each stage is completed in a set order (1) after the previous stage is complete (1). **(2)**

2. Analysis and research (1). Specification (1). Initial idea generation (1). **(3)**

3. Advantage: Clear what must be done and when (1).

   Advantage: Ensures each stage is complete before moving on (1).

   Disadvantage: Any *one* from: Lacks flexibility (1). Hinders creativity (1). Provides few opportunities for evaluation and improvement (1). **(6)**

Page 72 Design strategies: Iterative design

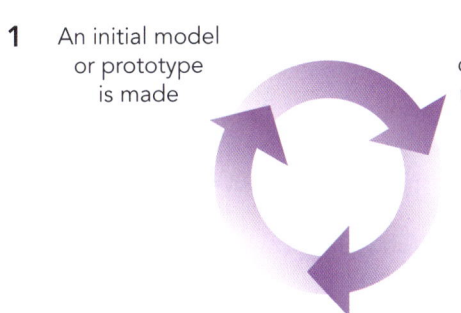

1. An initial model or prototype is made → This is tested to check how well it meets the needs of the user → The design is evaluated, and an improved iteration is made **(4)**

2. Any *two* from: Allows flexibility and creativity (2). Errors can be found and corrected quickly (2). More opportunities for testing and evaluation (2). **(4)**

3. An example may be graphic design or architecture (1); a designer may create an initial design, then show it to the customer and modify. This can happen many times before the final design of the product (1). In addition, modifications can then be made after the product is created (1). **(3)**

Page 73 Design strategies: Inclusive design

1.

Example of inclusive design	How it is inclusive
Toothbrush with curvy handle	Easy for children to hold
Large button telephone (1)	Easier for disabled and elderly to see and press keys (1)
Large button remote (1)	Easier for disabled and elderly to see and press keys (1)
Tin opener with large grip handles (1)	Easier for anyone to hold and use (1)

Any other similar answers. **(8)**

2. Advantages: Ensures design doesn't leave people out (1). Reduces user frustration if suits a wider range of users (1).

   Disadvantages: Increased cost for research and development (1). Increased time needed to get design correct for a wider target market (1). **(4)**

Page 74 Design strategies: User-centred design

1. User needs and wants **(1)**

2. At all stages **(1)**

3. It is too specialised to a specific user **(1)**

Page 74 Design strategies: Sustainable design

1. Non-renewable **(1)**

2. Any *two* from: Use renewable energy sources (1). Use recyclable materials (1). Design for repair and reuse (1). **(2)**

Page 75 Design strategies: Ergonomic design

1. More comfortable (1); Safer (1) **(2)**

2. (B) … interact with products. **(1)**

Answers: Workbook

Page 75 Iterative design: Analysis of the design brief

1. Any *one* from: Design a product that is fit for purpose (2). Know exactly what the brief is asking (2). **(2)**

Page 76 Iterative design: Methods of researching the product requirements

1. Primary (1); Secondary (1) **(2)**
2. Any *three* from: questionnaires (1); surveys (1); interviews (1); focus groups (1). **(3)**
3. Any *three* from: internet (1); books (1); magazines (1); data sheets (1); existing products (1); images (1); market research (1). **(3)**
4. Any *two* from: Can see how it is assembled (1). Can see the range of materials used (1). Can see how it functions (1). Can see how it meets the user's needs (1). *Any other relevant answer* (1). **(2)**
5. Data that gives you the average measurements for different parts of the body within different age ranges (1). Helps the designer make sure that their design will fit the target market (1). **(2)**

Page 77 Iterative design: Producing an engineering design specification

1. Any *three* from: cost (1); customer (1); environment (1); function (1); materials (1). **(3)**
2. Any *two* from: Ergonomic handle (1); Be reusable (1); Be correct size for an adult user (1); Be hygienic (1); *Any other relevant answer* (1). **(2)**

Page 77 Iterative design: Generating design ideas by sketching and modelling

1. modify (1); sketching (1) **(2)**

Page 78 Iterative design: Modelling ideas

1. Any *two* from: size (1); aesthetics (1); ergonomics (1); function (1). **(2)**
2. Virtual (1); Physical (1). **(2)**
3. Any *four* from: Design can be seen in 3D (1). Quicker to edit (1). Can be tested on screen (1). No modelling materials required (1). File can later be used for CAM (1). **(4)**
4. Any *two* from: clay (1); card (1); wood (1); 3D printed plastics (e.g. ABS, PLA) (1); breadboards (1). **(2)**
5. (C) … both full size and to scale. **(1)**
6. (B) The design is then modified. **(1)**
7. It can cost a lot of time and money to modify a design once the manufacturing process has started. (2)
   When picked up during the design stage, the modifications can be remodelled and tested to check that they are correct before the product is manufactured. (2) **(4)**

Page 79 Design criteria: Needs and wants

1. Any two from needs and wants (1); criteria from ACCESS FM (1), qualitative and quantitative criteria (1). **(2)**
2. Needs are what must be included for the product to function as intended (1). They are necessities (1). **(2)**
3. Wants are what research says users would like (1), but are not necessities required to have the correct function (1). **(2)**

Page 80 Design criteria: Quantitative and qualitative

1. User needs: any *three* suitable needs that people might have for a bike, such as: To have adjustable seat height with movement of 100 mm; Range of gears for ease of riding (1); Standard frame size (1); Lightweight frame (1).

User wants: any *three* suitable wants that people might have for a bike, such as: Padding in the saddle to keep rider comfortable; Range of colours (1); Weight (1); Accessories, such as lights (1). **(6)**

2   Quantitative (for example):
- Wheel size stated (1).
- Seat adjustment 100 mm (1).

Qualitative (for example):
- Material suggestion for frame (1).
- Suggested colour for the frame (1). **(4)**

Page 81 Design criteria: ACCESS FM

1   Suggested answers below. **(4)**

Customer	You need to know what age and gender you are designing for as this will affect the design (1).
	For example: An elderly user might need larger buttons to press (1).
Material	You need to know which materials you can and cannot use. Some might not be available (1).
	For example: A product for a child must use non-toxic and easy to clean materials such as plastics (1).

Page 81 Manufacturing considerations: Scale

1   **(A)** Football stadium **(1)**
2   **(B)** Screws **(1)**
3   **(C)** Bolts **(1)**
4   Wouldn't design something that has high production costs for mass production, this would impact on company profits (1). Scale would also impact on material choices, as mass produced items must use materials that are readily available (1). **(2)**

Page 82 Manufacturing considerations: Availability and form

1   Continuation of production – if batch or mass produced, materials must be available for all items (1). Lost production time if materials are not available (1). Raised cost of production if materials are not available (1). **(3)**

2   It is often more cost-effective to incorporate standard forms in a design (1). Simplicity when sourcing materials for manufacturing (1). **(2)**

Page 82 Manufacturing considerations: Processes

1   Answers shown below. **(4)**

Process	Description
Wasting	Cutting excess material away. (1)
Joining (1)	Soldering parts together.
Finishing (1)	Adding paint to a product.
Assembly	Screwing parts together to make a product. (1)

Page 83 Manufacturing considerations: Production costs

1
- Labour (1)
- Capital costs (1) **(2)**

2   So that the product does not make a loss when sold (1) or so that manufacturing costs are not more than the retail price (1). Long term costs can be taken into account as may be large capital costs that will be earned back over a longer period of time (1). **(3)**

Page 83 Influences on product design: Pull and push

1   a) Market pull (1)
    b) Technology push (1) **(2)**
2   Technology push **(1)**
3   Market pull **(1)**

Page 84 Influences on product design: Standards

1   British **(1)**
2   International (1) Organization (1); Standardization (1). **(3)**
3   a) United Kingdom Conformity Assessed **(1)**

Answers: Workbook   107

b) The mark tells customers that the product has been made to the required standards to be sold in the UK. It is safe and good quality. **(1)**

Page 85 Influences on product design: Legislation

1. A law that has been made an Act of Parliament (1). **(1)**

2. Prosecuted and fined or jailed **(1)**

3. Health and Safety at Work Act **(1)**

4. Companies must follow risk assessments to protect the workforce. This means that some design concepts can't be made if the process is not suitable and safe. Then any *two* from: The product must be designed to comply with health and safety laws (1). Users must be able to interact with the product safely (1). The legislation has been written to protect consumers using the product (1). **(3)**

Page 86 Influences on product design: Planned obsolescence

1.
   - Changes in users' needs or wants (1)
   - No longer does the job that it was made to do (1) **(2)**

2. It has a planned lifetime before it needs replacing **(1)**.

3. People will need to buy a new one **(1)**.

4. More waste as old products are disposed of (1). More materials and energy needed to make replacement products (1). **(2)**

Page 87 Influences on product design: Sustainable design and the circular economy

1. **(6)**

Rethink	Could the product be made using different materials? (1)
Reuse	Use a product for another purpose. (1)
Recycle	Is it easy for the materials to be separated for recycling? (1)
Repair	Save the user money by mending an item.
Reduce	Make a durable product that doesn't need to be replaced quickly. (1)
Refuse	Decline to use a non-sustainable material. (1)

2.
   - Produce the product (1).
   - Use the product (1).
   - Recycle the product (1). **(3)**

Page 88 Types of drawing

1. Any *one* from:
   - quick to produce ideas **(1)**
   - no special equipment needed. **(1)**

2. Vertical lines (1); 30° angles (1); overall shape (1). **(3)**

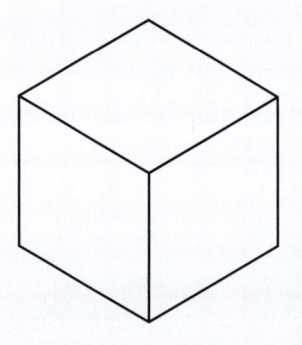

3. Isometric shows three sides of a product in 3D (1) OR Oblique only shows two sides in 3D as the front is still in 2D (1). **(1)**

4. (C) … an exploded view. **(1)**

5. (B) … what parts of the product will look like when they are assembled. **(1)**

6. *One* mark for each part correctly added; maximum 4 marks: two horizontal arrows, one rectangle, and one feedback loop. **(4)**

7. *One* mark for each correct shape and name: left to right: Start/End; Decision; Process or Task). **(3)**

8. (A) … standard symbols. **(1)**

9. (C) Wiring diagram **(1)**

Page 90 Working drawings: Third angle orthographic projection and standard conventions

1. Any *two* from: part name (1); drawing number (1); scale (1); tolerance (1); materials (1); finishes (1). **(2)**

2. **(B)** The drawing has been accurately enlarged or reduced compared with the part to make the picture fit the paper. **(1)**

3. **(A)** 34.8 mm and **D** 35.2 mm **(2)**

4. Correct drawing of circle and trapezoid (1); correct order (circle before trapezoid) (1). **(2)**

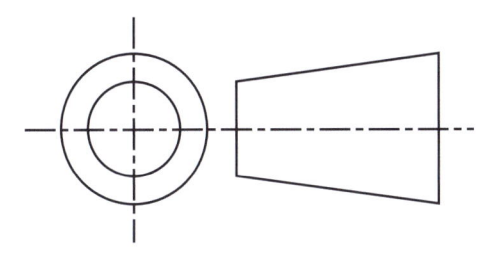

Page 91 Working drawings: Dimensions

1. 70 on height, with double-headed arrow (1); 160 on length, with double-headed arrow (1); R20 pointing to circle (1) **(3)**

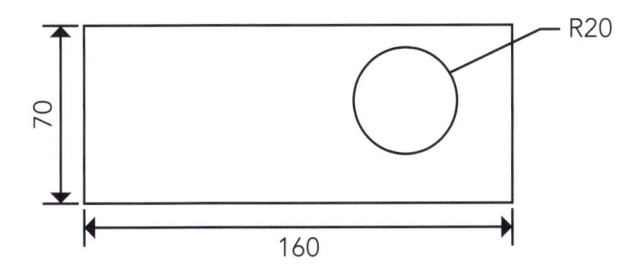

Page 91 Working drawings: Line types

1. Answers shown in table. **(3)**

Outline	———————————— (1)
Centre line	—·—·—·—·—·—·— (1)
Hidden detail	·············· (1)

Page 91 Working drawings: Abbreviations

1. Answers shown in table. **(5)**

Abbreviation	Definition
DIA	Diameter (1)
MATL	Material (1)
DRG	Drawing
SQ (1)	Square
AF	Across Flats (1)
CL (1)	Centre Line

Page 92 Working drawings: Mechanical features

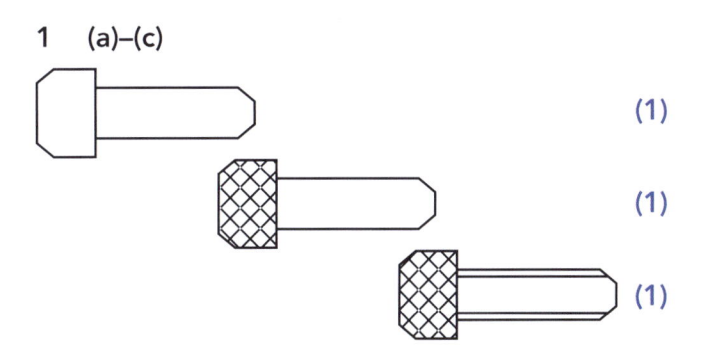

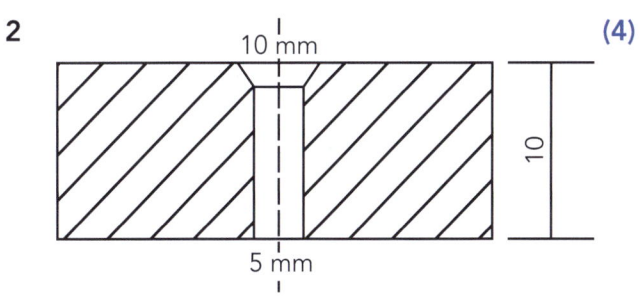

1. (a)–(c)

   (1)
   (1)
   (1)

2. **(4)** 10 mm, 5 mm, 10

Page 93 Using CAD drawing software

1. Using CAD software, a designer can share their design ideas with other people quickly and easily. This allows others to collaborate on the design. Then, any *three* from: Once a design has been drawn on screen in 3D (1) it can be viewed from all directions (1).

   Easy to make changes or edit design (1) without needing to restart the drawing again (1). **(4)**

2. Any *two* from: Can be easily edited (1); Can be used later to create the file that the CAM machine can use to make it (1); Can quickly change the finish of the design to see how it

Answers: Workbook 109

looks (1); Can test the product onscreen by assembling different parts (1). **(2)**

3 Any *two* from: Difficulties getting ideas onscreen can limit creativity (1); Need training to use the software successfully (1); Need to have a computer and CAD software (1); Time consuming compared with sketching (1). **(2)**

Page 94 Evaluating design ideas

1 Helps visualise the design (1); Allow hands-on testing (1). **(2)**

2 Design brief (1) and specification (1). **(2)**

3 Description including:

Create a score (1). Structure to evaluate against so all ideas are evaluated against same points (1). Gives criteria to test against (1). **(3)**

4 Any *two* from:

Puts the users' needs into points that the design idea can be checked against (1). Can use a ranking table (matrix) to help evaluate the idea (1). Can be used throughout the design and make process to continually check that the product will meet the requirements (1). **(2)**

Page 95 Modelling methods

1 **(B)** CAD and **(C)** Block **(2)**

2 Any *two* advantages from: Easily edited (1); File can be used later to make model via CAM or produce file for manufacture (1); Allows design to be seen from all angles (1); Onscreen parts can be assembled to check fit (1); Can be modelled on screen rendered in the correct material (1).

Any *two* disadvantages from: Need a skilled designer to use software (1); Takes time to produce detailed designs (1); Can't physically hold the model and check measurements and ergonomics (1); CAD software can be expensive to purchase (1). **(4)**

3 Electronic circuits **(1)**

4 Any *two* from: sizes (1); fit with other parts (1), ergonomic fit (1); visual of all parts of design (1). **(2)**

5 Any *one* advantage from: No specialist equipment (1); Quick (1); Allows sizes to be checked (1); Gives a visual of the design in 3D (1).

Any *one* disadvantage from: Limits to the detail that can be modelled (1); Hard to model functioning parts (1). **(4)**

Page 96 Evaluating design outcomes

1 Micrometer (1). Steel ruler (1). **(2)**

2 Numerical factual data **(1)**

3 Design can be checked against data that was set by the client (1). Result can be analysed to identify specific improvement areas (1). Can check against measurements stated in the specification that need to be accurate (1). **(3)**

4 Any *two* benefits from: Physical model gives testers a clear view of all sides and features (1); Can hold, touch, and test for function and size (1); Parts can be fitted to other parts to check for fit and function (1).

Any *two* limitations from: Not all detail may be shown depending on the modelling method (1); Some testing might not be possible depending on the model type (1); Testing could be random if there is no structure of things to test and feedback (1). **(4)**

5 Other people can spot issues with the design that the designer may not have identified (1).

If the design is not fit for purpose it will not be a success when made into a product (1).

Changes at the design stage cost a lot less than changes made once the product has gone to manufacture (1).

Most designs are not perfect first time and need refinement – feedback from an evaluation will make the modifications easier by guiding the designer (1). provide technical information required by manufacturers to make the product **(4)**

Acknowledgements

The authors and publishers acknowledge the following sources of copyright material and are grateful for the permissions granted. While every effort has been made, it has not always been possible to identify the sources of all the material used, or to trace all copyright holders. If any omissions are brought to our notice, we will be happy to include the appropriate acknowledgements on reprinting.

Thanks to the following for permission to reproduce images:

Cover Talaj/GI; Inside Science & Society Picture Library/GI; Michael Reeve/GI; Morsa Images/GI; Westend61/GI; Sergii Iaremenko/Science Photo Library/GI; Westend61/GI; Compassionate Eye Foundation/Robert Daly/GI; John Rensten/GI; Designer/GI; Rakdee/GI; Rambo182/GI; Alexandre Morin-Laprise/GI; Kurtcan/GI; Monty Rakusen/GI; Volodymyr Kalyniuk/GI; Gorodenkoff/GI; Ugde/GI; Rost-9D/GI; Bakhtiar_Zein/GI(X2); Shana Novak/GI; Benito Catudio/GI; Peter Cade/GI; Papakon Mitsanit/GI; www.flickr.Com/Photos/Jeijiang/GI; BSI Kitemark logo is used with permission from the British Standards Institution; UKCA mark from www.gov.uk/guidance/using-the-ukca-marking; CE Symbol from https://ec.europa.eu/growth/single-market/ce-marking_en; The ISO logo is reproduced with the permission of the International Organization for Standardization, ISO. Copyright remains with ISO; Fiordaliso/GI; Philippe Turpin/GI; Marina Dekhnik/GI; Chaosamran_Studio/GI; Pramote Polyamate/GI; Anilyanik/GI; Monty Rakusen/GI; Naftizin/GI; Romieg/GI; Nitat Termmee/GI; Pasieka/GI; Jag Images/GI; Image Source/GI; Tara Moore/GI; Nadezhda Kozhedub/GI; Gorodenkoff/GI; Jeffrey Coolidge/GI; poba/GI; Golubovy/GI; Vm/GI; Andrew Brookes/GI; Andreypopov/GI; Witthaya Prasongsin/GI; Sean Gladwell/GI; Lucianojoaquim/GI; Flavio Coelho/GI; Digital quiz: Anilyanik/GI

Key: GI = Getty Images